Security from the South: Intersections of Religion, Gender, and Race
Edited by Samar Al-Bulushi, Sahana Ghosh, and Inderpal Grewal

Security from the South

Postcolonial and Imperial Entanglements

Samar Al-Bulushi, Sahana Ghosh, and Inderpal Grewal

Recent elections globally have been marked by security discourses backed by a resurgent militarism. In Brazil, Jair Bolsonaro drew on his military background to form a governing alliance of militarized actors and Pentecostal conservatives in 2018. In India, Narendra Modi won the 2019 prime ministerial election by calling himself the "watchman" of the nation, leading the resurgence of a militant Hinduism. In Kenya, Uhuru Kenyatta and William Ruto framed the 2013 elections in religio-political narratives of redemption, offering the nation a chance to be "born again," and to free itself from the horrors of the 2007–8 election violence.[1] Meanwhile in the United States, the slogan "America First" came to represent Donald Trump's brand of white supremacy, with Trump emerging as the quintessential patriarchal authority claiming to protect American families from purported threats posed by migrants and terrorists. All of these leaders, among many others, are men whose relationship to religious, corporate, and militarized masculinity is central to their authority.[2] In short, political leaders across the world, largely men, have become entangled in distinct yet connected forms of political and moral authority that legitimize and sustain gendered, sexualized, and racialized logics of militarism and policing.

This special issue critically reflects on security regimes—and their effects and entanglements—across the world, particularly as they rely on forms of authority that draw from gendered, racial, and religious movements. At stake is the question whether it is possible to conceive of security as one monolithic system or, instead, as a series of interlinked and mutually reinforcing regimes. While we emphasize the significance of shared logics of rule, we are skeptical of singular understandings or frames.[3] We

DOI 10.1215/01642472-9771021   © 2022 Duke University Press

1

ground our inquiry not only in empirical studies in/of the Global South but also in a commitment to explore epistemologies and concepts that emerge from these contexts. Deploying a transnational feminist approach, we capture the *fluidity* between supposedly separate scales (e.g., North/ South, intimate/global, etc.) at which religion, gender, and race operate.[4] While we are interested in interconnections between seemingly discrete populations and territories, security from the South as a method and as an analytic suggests that it is not possible to speak of one overarching set of politics, practices, and ideas that constitute security regimes today. Instead, in tracing the colonial continuities, the imperial geographies, and the forms of difference through which people become subjects of, resist, and shore up security regimes, we insist on a pluriversal lens onto a world in which "security" appears beguilingly universal.[5]

The essays in this issue track the place of difference in the making of, and resistance to, security logics and modes of rule. From everyday policing to counterinsurgency and drone warfare, we approach "security" as a logic of power. We understand governance related to security to mean a preoccupation with *threat* posed by purportedly suspicious "others," a project that connects family and community to the state, private companies, and international bodies.

The project of security has taken on affective dimensions, becoming a formidable tool for mobilizing fears, and making emotion central to the cultivation of national attachments as well as exclusions.[6] In this sense, "security" is something lived and felt as much as it is a policy or institutional practice—whether by those on the receiving end of policing and war, or by "citizen forces" who take on the mantle of vigilance.[7]

The "Global South" as a Field of Power

How does the "Global South" as a field of power, linked to multiple and layered imperial histories, shed light on the changing articulations of security today? In the 1930s, Antonio Gramsci and W. E. B. Du Bois were among the first to employ the idea of "South" to capture uneven relations of power.[8] By the end of the twentieth century, in the aftermath of the Cold War, the term *Global South* has continued to offer a critical alternative to the flattening and homogenizing notion of globalization.[9] Academics and activists alike have employed vocabularies of North/South and core/ periphery to refer to uneven patterns of wealth across broad regions, and to emphasize the continued relevance of histories of colonialism for our understandings of geopolitical power relations and persisting inequalities. Within mainstream North American policy and academic circles, regions of the Global South are often preemptively diagnosed as threatening geographies. In what Junaid Rana refers to as "racialized regionalisms," policymakers and their "expert" counterparts in the US academy imagine different countries as a single geopolitical mass, producing arguments about regional exceptionalism that are then used to justify foreign intervention.[10]

Critical scholarship on security and securitization remains focused primarily on the project of US empire, or more broadly, on the hegemonic military powers of the Global North that aim to control national borders and the flow of capital. Despite the richness of this material, one of the risks is that we are left with reified conceptualizations of empire as a singular, totalizing force, accompanied with spatially predetermined centers and recipients of imperial power. This, as Ella Shohat reminds us, presupposes neat binaries of East vs. West and North vs. South and "ironically repositions whiteness and Westerners as a normative interlocutor."[11] In this context, regions in the Global South are analyzed *only* in relation to US interests. Global South states are conceptualized merely as "proxies," or as passive recipients of "global" designs, wherein they are positioned geographically outside of the "global."[12]

Importantly, the conceptual binarism (North/South, etc.) that Shohat describes also contributes to a bypassing of those who do not fit neatly into either category, especially as states that fall within the "Global South" of American security empire are key enactors of security regimes influential in their respective regions. Think India or Kenya. While some of the essays contained here (particularly those on India by Sahana Ghosh and by Inderpal Grewal, Dipin Kaur, and Sasha Sabherwal; and on Kenya by Samar Al-Bulushi) direct analytical attention to the histories and practices of Global South security states, the issue as a whole interrogates the boundedness of the category of the "Global South" itself, resisting the notion that it refers to a fixed geography. We scrutinize the politics of geohistorical categories wherein the world map is divided into distinct territories and regions that signify difference.[13] We work alongside those scholars who have traced the various ways in which the peoples and places "of" the Global South have always been transnational, not confined to any one region or formally defined territory.[14] They illustrate that contemporary imperial formations are informed and shaped by pre- and postcolonial repertoires of rule, and that diasporic populations now living in what is known as the Global North are increasingly entwined in these very imperial formations.

The essays are therefore most compelled by the notion of complicated itineraries rather than unidirectional flows, and do not insist on an already-determined "revolutionary subject" as a prerequisite for feminist analysis.[15] We are reluctant to conceive of the "South" only through the lens of emancipation—as this comes with the risk of mystification and romanticization—and are attentive to actors and practices that simultaneously challenge and reinscribe hegemonic power relations.[16] Some essays feature actors who would be considered problematic from the standpoint of liberation politics. Both Deborah A. Thomas and Negar Razavi, for example, shed light on diasporic experts who in many ways make possible the forms of power that police the South, showing how those identified as coming from the "South" become complicit in reproducing knowledge about the South. As Thomas probes in her piece: how should we understand diasporic actors who occupy a subaltern position as racial minorities in the United States, but who wield considerable power returning to Global South security states? Is it sufficient to conceive of them as an extension of imperial power emanating from the Global North? Such figures, in many ways, constitute the "other" of leftist analysis and critique. They are both positioned as Global South actors while also politically other than the authentic, revolutionary subject imagined by Global North leftists. If "Security from the South" complicates such separations of North from South, perhaps the most radical reorientation that we invite is to ask where the "heart" of empire is. Razavi's essay about the transnational networks of funding and knowledge making that dominate US policy making on security prompts critical questions about how a seemingly distant "Middle East" operates within the heart of Washington, DC, as influential Gulf states attempt to shape the direction of US foreign policy.

Militarized mapping exercises inscribe and reify dominant modes of geographic thought, delineating North and South, "native," and "foreign." Logics of contradistinction form the core of securitized rule (Ghosh, this issue), fixing subjects and states in place through gendered, racialized, and religious modes of differentiation. These discrete geographies of imagination foreclose consideration of alternative mapping practices, "many of which were/are produced outside the tenets of official cartography: fugitive and maroon maps, literacy maps, food-nourishment maps, family maps, music maps."[17] This issue brings into dialogue people, places, and politics seldom considered alongside one another—from residents of India's increasingly securitized yet "friendly" border with Bangladesh, to Arab and Iranian American security "experts" in Washington, DC, to the African troops and political elites who co-constitute geographies of global warfare. In doing so, we aim to analyze the varied logics of security regimes in a transnational context. We embrace both temporal and spatial promiscuity in the interest of theorizing security *across* divergent temporalities and spatialities.

A Transnational Feminist Approach to Security Imperialism

How might we capture the power of security as the dominant force organizing social life today without reifying it as a monolithic system *or* forestalling the possibility of developing a critical analysis that is attentive to connections across time and space? The contributors to this issue recognize that US hegemony extends to the university, such that the domain of critical security studies is preoccupied primarily with the workings of US empire. As women of color based in the Global North, we are attuned to the complexities of distance and proximity as we inhabit multiple locations and commitments. Like other feminist scholars, it is a consciousness of the politics of location that guides the questions we ask and the connections we make,[18] cognizant that we are "equally accountable to unequal places."[19]

When one considers the US government's export of ideologies and technologies of policing and militarism abroad, the term *national security state* fails to sufficiently account for its transnational and imperial dimensions.[20] Yet while the United States is a hegemonic imperial formation, it is augmented, sustained, and sometimes in conflict with other hegemons (e.g., China, Russia) and regional strongmen (e.g., Kenya, Saudi Arabia, India), each with their own universalizing imaginaries. Our conceptualization of security imperialism is therefore attentive to multiple, overlapping circulations. "Communities in large swaths of the world," as Al-Bulushi, Ghosh, and Tahir argue, "survive a multiscalar pluriverse of power and politics. These gritty relations have histories and imaginaries that intersect with but are not reducible to the imaginative and historical landscapes of the United States."[21] Consequently, we neither decenter the United States in favor of a seemingly external "local," nor do we approach the study of other regions as simply the products of US influence. Thinking *across* time and space allows for consideration of the ways in which US empire has shaped practices elsewhere, but not in isolation, not without tension, and not without links to other empires. It also allows us to move *beyond* the US sphere of influence to consider histories that emerge from before American empire, and before its recent "global war on terror."

"Security from the South" thus encompasses imperial "war on terror" projects, but asserts a before and after to such projects, as security regimes across the Global South are enmeshed in longer histories of colonialism and racisms, religion, and gender/sexuality. Contemporary anxieties about minority populations—be they gendered/sexual, religious, or racial—are not new but are the product of interactions between old histories and new provocations.[22] As sovereignty is increasingly defined by security in the form of surveillance and militarized policing, religion, gender, and race are newly entangled in the production of divergent modes of power. We therefore foreground fluidity and multiplicity rather than coherence and unity.

To this end, our interest in processes of racialization is one that is attentive both to historical specificities, and to historically changing intersections and entanglements. We emphasize the structuring role of race and white supremacy in histories of colonial rule, dispossession, and extraction, noting the centrality of surveillance and policing to the production of difference. Logics of preemption in particular constitute multi-scalar modes of racialization that are simultaneously enacted within US policing practices at home and war making abroad.[23] At the same time, we are cognizant of what Anjali Arondekar refers to as "the invisible nationalism that undergirds most discussions of racial formations" in the United States.[24] A relational framework allows for consideration of how the race concept assumes different meanings in dialogue with scattered hegemonies.[25] The essays are attentive to the varying meanings and politics of Blackness, Islam, and Sikhism in different times and places, broadening our understandings of race and racialization beyond Eurocentric anxieties and teleologies.

The current wave of techno-fetishism among scholars in the Global North—particularly in relation to drones—conjures images of advanced technologies that are seemingly inaccessible across much of the Global South, all the while obscuring more mundane, but equally invasive, low-tech modes of monitoring and control on which the more technologically advanced modes remain reliant.[26] With this in mind, the essay by Al-Bulushi asks us what it would mean to provincialize the imperial war room. If we are indeed committed to making sense of the infrastructures of endless war, Al-Bulushi argues, it seems that we must contend with other war rooms, and this may demand a different set of maps. A transnational feminist lens exhorts us to illuminate the binary that is produced and is at stake here: the production of the Kenyan street as the feminine/local on which the masculine/global of drone warfare is being enacted.[27] As with the diasporic circulations and investments in multiple security states, security from the South reveals such entanglements, produced as separations, as heres and theres.

Gender and Religion

Our transnational feminist approach is attuned to the intersection of gender and religion in the logic of security regimes. While the critical scholarship on security and militarization have paid attention to its gendered, racial, and cultural aspects, attention to the role of religion and religious identity has been rare.[28] The production of religious gendered subjects has long been central to colonial power, to nationalisms (imperial and post-colonial), and to security regimes. From the politics of "saving Muslim women" to "security feminisms," the gendering of religious identities as instruments and targets of security regimes cannot be underestimated.[29] Security regimes incorporate gendered and racialized experts into the security establishment while also offering practitioners heteronormative potentialities of power.[30] Sahana Ghosh's essay, in particular, reveals how the maintenance of "peace" by the Indian security forces at its border with Bangladesh is carried out through heteropatriarchal modes of disciplining and silencing the Muslim and lower-caste citizens of the borderlands. Religion and heteropatriarchy work together to shore up the legitimacy of the security state and renew the minoritization of its border subjects.

When we decenter 9/11 as *the* defining turning point for the rise of "security," we disrupt linear trajectories and allow for the rhizomatic ways in which the religious past appears in the present. Egypt, for example, enacted emergency laws long before 9/11 under the pretext of defending against religious violence. Meanwhile, Grewal, Kaur, and Sabherwal capture India's long history of painting Sikhs as violent militants, one that builds on a longer history—both colonial and precolonial—of religious identity as a racial project and also as a revolutionary formation.

Such colonial-racial logics of rule have continued into the postcolonial state. As Ghosh notes in her essay, Muslim communities in India are differently racialized and differentially constituted as minority citizens in a polity being reshaped along Hindu supremacist lines. In this sense, Kenya (Al-Bulushi), Egypt, and India, as well as Caribbean countries such as Jamaica, represent alternative itineraries to those offered by theorists of a US-led security empire, as security states across the Global South have long worked to shape ideas about the relationship between religion and "proper" uses of violence, designating state-sanctioned violence as legitimate (Thomas).

Purportedly secular states like the United States often conceive of religion as a political determinant of militarism and violence. Scholars like Saba Mahmood have examined how states manage religious ideology and practice, often by promoting religious "reform" in the name of peace and security.[31] A rich body of work has traced the various ways in which surveillance and securitization have criminalized and queered the practice and identification with Islam in relation to the war on terror.[32] It has also provided critical perspectives on the reconfigurations of citizenship as/of minorities at the intersections of race and religion.[33] As the essays in this issue show, religion is deployed by security states in a number of ways: to create internal Others of the nation only to be tenuously included (Ghosh), to establish forms of moral authority that mobilize voting publics and consolidate majoritarian publics (Al-Bulushi; Grewal, Kaur, and Sabherwal) or to reify and racialize external threats through Islamophobia (Razavi).

"Security from the South" also raises questions about the liberal recognition of protests and disruptions in relation to security (in particular Ghosh; Thomas; Razavi). The issue draws attention to the multiple affective lives of security, some that turn up cracks in the hegemonic state story, some others that foreground contradictory diasporic and illiberal attachments. We emphasize the importance of being attuned to the ways in which religion, race, and gender articulate together in specific historical contexts. At the same time, these essays consider the religious underpinnings of security states, alerting us to the various ways in which authoritarian regimes allied to particular religious reform movements are displacing liberal-democratic modes of rule. Our use of transnational feminist approaches that critique such secular-liberal exceptionalism then enables us to suggest sovereignty's own fissures or multiplicities (Thomas) as much as it does the postcolonial state's ongoing engagements with gendered forms of religious and state authority.

At the broadest level, we explore how *difference* (religion, gender, race), a central project of the modern security state, articulates and operates within and through security regimes, through policies of "inclusion," or exclusion, minoritization, or outright targeting that ultimately reproduce and entrench forms of hierarchy, exclusion, and sovereignty. A transnational feminist lens enables us to read seemingly unified security regimes otherwise, demanding conceptual reorientations in order to take seriously disruption and difference.

A Pluriversal Lens

The first set of essays (Thomas; Al-Bulushi; Grewal, Kaur, and Sabherwal) remind us that we need to look beyond the Global North as the formative impetus for a new politics of "security" as well as its discontents. Focused on the regulation and surveillance of Black bodies in the Tivoli Gardens neighborhood of Kingston, Jamaica, Deborah Thomas probes the project of security in a context where police violence and extrajudicial killings are not typically seen as part of the global phenomenon of anti-Black racism. We learn about the Jamaican Diaspora Crime Intervention and Prevention Task Force (JDCIPT), which brings the expertise of Jamaicans living in the diaspora to bear on security issues within Jamaica. What sense can we make of these diasporic actors' own imbrication in the protection of whiteness, class hierarchy, and heteropatriarchy? Thomas illustrates how postcolonial sovereignty is as much the product of diasporic practices as it is the product of the seemingly bounded political formation we continue to call the "state." The role of this diasporic foundation in shaping practices related to security in Jamaica complicates our understanding of the imperial circuits through which militarized approaches to "security" are taken up.

The essay by Samar Al-Bulushi approaches the war on terror not as one single apparatus of rule, but as a series of interrelated geopolitical projects. Against the Eurocentric, heteronormative paradigms that continue to structure analysis about post-9/11 global warfare, Al-Bulushi pushes us to decenter the view from the imperial war room, illustrated most poignantly in the 2016 thriller *Eye in the Sky*. Emphasizing the mutually constitutive relationship between Black spatial knowledge and geographies of domination,[34] her essay takes seriously the African subjects who co-constitute geographies of war making in East Africa today, from the political and business elite who normalize militarized masculinities and femininities, to the African troops whose affective and violent labor sustains war making in Somalia.

The essay by Grewal, Kaur, and Sabherwal insists on the continued relevance of histories of colonial militarism, postcolonial counterinsurgency and securitization, and traces how these sediment, surfacing in affective and material ways to radically alter both the state and minority populations. Focusing on the Indian state's counterinsurgent practices in Punjab in the 1980s and 1990s, much before the US-led global war on terror, the essay illustrates how Sikh masculinities change from the colonial to the postcolonial period in response to the anxieties of postcolonial territorial uncertainty. They argue that "security from the South" must also engage with the violent aftermath of colonial partitioning—the divisions of nation-states created by colonial rule, and the subjects formed by older and newer forms of power. The authors approach the targeting of Sikhs as part of the process of postcolonial nation making through militarism and security of border regions that alters its patriarchies. The essay traces continuities of masculine power from the colonial to the postcolonial period that are in dialogue with broader geopolitical dynamics and across different scales. The postcolonial state's engagement with the US-led global war on terror has reanimated narratives about Sikh insurgents as "terrorists." The emergence of new securitized patriarchies in South Asia can neither be reduced to, nor entirely divorced from the geopolitics of this global war.

The second set of essays (Ghosh; Razavi) explore the significance of affect for regimes of security. While scholars have written extensively about the politics of fear, these authors turn our attention to other affective realms. For Ghosh, the cultivation and management of emotion—specifically, the discursive construction of the notion of a "friendly" border—is central to the security project. Razavi draws our attention to diasporic security experts in Washington, DC, who draw on multiple affective registers to influence the range of stakeholders that make up the US security establishment, from powerful Middle Eastern governments to different segments of their own diasporic communities to various factions within the white imperial security community. The essay points to the ways that difference—racial, diasporic—operates *within* the security state and constitute the empire's racial, religious imaginaries.

Sahana Ghosh takes us to South Asia and the politics of legibility and protest in relation to the affective economies of national security. She turns our attention to a clash between residents of India's eastern borderlands and the national Border Security Forces along the "friendly" India-Bangladesh border to analyze the soft violence of security regimes and the disruptions to them. Ghosh argues that the Indian state relies on heteropatriarchal gender norms and the discourse of family to produce unequal, minority citizens and secure their subordinated inclusion. Reading the illegible political potency of humiliation otherwise, the essay tracks the fate of cracks and fissures in the affective economy of "friendliness" of this border security regime and shows how the intersection of gender and religious identity is foundational to its continuing coherence, power, and endurance.

Razavi's essay illustrates how the "South" as diasporic positionality operates in the proverbial heart of empire. She directs our attention to a small but growing number of security experts "from" the diasporic communities of the Middle East who engage in a multiplicity of affective practices as they navigate competing interests in Washington, DC, from the Arab and Israeli governments who fund US think tanks to US government officials, to their own familial and social networks back "home" in the Middle East as well as their diasporic communities in the United States. In doing so, she argues that these are ideal political actors through which to trace how geopolitical rivalries *within* the Middle East shape what is understood to be a homogenous and rational US security state, illustrating how the "Middle East" is imagined and operationalized within the security imaginary of Washington. Razavi's essay thus destabilizes dominant modes of geographic thought that simultaneously reify images of a seemingly coherent and unified US empire, and that conceive of "Washington, DC," and the "Middle East" as discrete geographies.

It is time to think anew the universalism of security imperialism through the pluriversal lens of the Global South as a field of power, and as a space of difference produced through power. By attending to transnational histories and entanglements, this issue looks beyond conceptions of "security" that analytically limit dynamics of securitization either to a homogenizing influence, or to an imperial effect wherein technologies and ideas flow from North to South. Our commitment to contingency, fluidity, and multiplicity is accompanied by a commitment to solidarity across time and space. It is precisely by attending to intersecting forms of power that we can piece together the infrastructures that sustain projects of "security" on the one hand, and explore new modes of living on the other. These modes of living—in many cases, of simply getting by—raise new questions about care and safety in contexts of political uncertainty and precarity. A focus on the mundane, where everyday modes of survival are often productive of rupture and repair, seems just as important.

Samar Al-Bulushi is assistant professor of anthropology at the University of California, Irvine. Her published work has appeared in *American Anthropologist*, *Cultural Dynamics*, and *Security Dialogue*, and she has written for public outlets including *Africa Is a Country*, *Jacobin*, and *Warscapes*.

Sahana Ghosh is assistant professor of anthropology at the National University of Singapore. Her work on militarization, gender, borderlands, and the politics of mobility within South Asia has been published in *American Anthropologist*, *Comparative Studies of South Asia, Africa, and the Middle East*, and *Gender, Place, and Culture*, among others. Her work has also been published in public outlets such as *Border Criminologies*, *The Conversation*, and *Café Dissensus*.

Inderpal Grewal is professor emerita in the Program in Women's, Gender, and Sexuality Studies at Yale University. She is a theorist of transnational feminism, focusing on imperialism, culture, and postcoloniality. The author and coeditor of many articles and several books and monographs, most recently *Saving the Security State: Exceptional Citizens in Twenty-First-Century America* (2017), she is currently working on projects addressing security regimes in the Global South and the resurgence of patriarchal authoritarian governments and anti-Muslim violence in India, and on masculinity and bureaucracy.

Notes

The authors would like to thank the *Social Text* collective, especially Jayna Brown, Tavia Nyong'o, and Marie Buck, for their engagement with and support of this special issue. We are grateful to the reviewers and to Madiha Tahir, Catherine Sameh, Laura Kang, and Deborah Thomas for their helpful feedback on early drafts of the introduction. We thank the Luce Foundation and Toby Volkmann for their support of the project that led to this special issue.

1. See Deacon, "Driving the Devil Out."

2. See I. Grewal, "Authoritarian Patriarchy and Its Populism."

3. See I. Grewal, *Saving the Security State*; Stoler, "Colonial Toxicities"; Besteman, *Militarized Global Apartheid*. As Inderpal Grewal observes, "The US imperial state is different in scale and in the nature of its exceptionalism." I. Grewal, *Saving the Security State*, 8.

4. We are inspired by the important feminist interventions on the politics of scale and interconnection in Massey, *For Space*; Mountz and Hyndman, "Feminist Approaches to the Global Intimate"; Smith, *Intimate Geopolitics*; Ali, *Delusional States*; Carby, *Imperial Intimacies*; Lowe, *Intimacies of Four Continents*.

5. For more on pluriversal epistemologies, see Ndlovu-Gatsheni, "Decoloniality as the Future"; Escobar, *Pluriversal Politics*.

6. See Lutz and Abu-Lughod, *Language and the Politics of Emotion*.

7. Akarsu, "Citizen Forces"; I. Grewal, *Saving the Security State*; Ghertner, McFann, and Goldstein, *Futureproof*.

8. Gramsci was interested in Northern Italy's colonial relation to Southern Italy, while Du Bois was interested in Jim Crow–era segregation in the United States. Gramsci, *Prison Notebooks*; Du Bois, *Black Reconstruction in America*.

9. Dados and Connell, "Global South."

10. See Rana, *Terrifying Muslims*; Abboud et al., "Towards a Beirut School"; Andersson, *No Go World*.

11. Shohat, "Area Studies," 69.

12. See Amar, *Security Archipelago*.

13. Coronil, "Beyond Occidentalism."

14. See, e.g., Lowe, *Intimacies of Four Continents*; Ho, *Graves of Tarim*.

15. Abu-Lughod, "Romance of Resistance"; Pratt, *Embodying Geopolitics*.

16. See especially I. Grewal and Kaplan, "Global Identities."

17. McKittrick, "On Plantations," 949.

18. I. Grewal and Kaplan, "Transnational Feminist Practices"; Lorde, *Sister/Outsider*; Perera and Razack, *At the Limits of Justice*.

19. John, *Discrepant Dislocations*, 4.

20. See Mountz "Where Asylum Seekers Wait"; Gonzalez, *Securing Paradise*; Schober, *Base Encounters*; I. Grewal, *Saving the Security State*; Loyd and Mountz, *Boats, Borders, and Bases*; Schrader, *Badges without Borders*.

21. Al-Bulushi, Ghosh, and Tahir, "American Anthropology."

22. Appadurai, *Fear of Small Numbers*.

23. Miller, "Data-Driven Policing and the Colonial Database."

24. Arondekar, "Geopolitics Alert!," 238–39.

25. Clarke and Thomas, *Globalization and Race*; Bacchetta, Maira, and Winant, "Global Raciality"; Molina and Ho Sang, introduction.

26. Donovan, Frowd, and Martin, "Introduction"; Parks and Kaplan, "Life in the Age of Drone Warfare"; Tahir, "Containment Zone"; Ghosh, "Everything Must Match."

27. Freeman, "Is Local : Global."

28. See, e.g., González, Gusterson, and Houtman, *Militarization*.

29. Abu-Lughod, *Do Muslim Women Need Saving?*; I. Grewal, *Saving the Security State*.

30. Razavi, "NatSec Feminism"; Al-Bulushi, "#SomeoneTellCNN"; O'Neill, "Soul of Security."

31. Mahmood, *"Secularism, Hermeneutics and Empire"*; Moallem, *Between Warrior Brother*.

32. Ahmad, "Homeland Insecurities"; Z. Grewal, *Islam Is a Foreign Country*; Maira, *Missing*; Maira, *9/11 Generation*; Puar and Rai, "Monster, Terrorist, Fag"; Rana, *Terrifying Muslims*.

33. I. Grewal, "Transnational America"; Johnson "African Americans."

34. McKittrick, *Demonic Grounds*.

References

Abboud, Samer, Omar S. Dahi, Waleed Hazbun, Nicole Sunday Grove, Coralie Pison Hindawi, Jamil Mouawad, and Sami Hermez. "Towards a Beirut School of Critical Security Studies." *Critical Studies on Security* 6, no. 3 (2018): 273–95.

Abu-Lughod, Lila. *Do Muslim Women Need Saving?* Cambridge, MA: Harvard University Press, 2013.

Abu-Lughod, Lila. "The Romance of Resistance: Tracing Transformations of Power through Bedouin Women." *American Ethnologist* 17, no. 1 (1990): 41–55.

Ahmad, Muneer. "Homeland Insecurities: Racial Violence the Day after September 11." *Social Text*, no. 72 (2002): 101–15.

Akarsu, Hayal. "Citizen Forces: The Politics of Community Policing in Turkey." *American Ethnologist* 47, no. 1 (2020): 27–42.

Al-Bulushi, Samar. "#SomeoneTellCNN: Cosmopolitan Militarism in the East African Warscape." *Cultural Dynamics* 31, no. 4 (2019): 323–49.

Al-Bulushi, Samar, Sahana Ghosh, and Madiha Tahir. "American Anthropology, Decolonization, and the Politics of Location." *American Anthropologist*, September 22, 2020. https://www.americananthropologist.org/commentaries/al-bulushi-ghosh-and-tahir.

Ali, Nosheen. *Delusional States: Feeling Rule and Development in Pakistan's Northern Frontier.* Cambridge: Cambridge University Press, 2019.

Amar, Paul. *The Security Archipelago: Human Security States, Sexuality Politics, and the End of Neoliberalism.* Durham, NC: Duke University Press, 2013.

Andersson, Ruben. *No Go World: How Fear Is Redrawing Our Maps and Infecting Our Politics.* Oakland: University of California Press, 2019.

Appadurai, Arjun. *Fear of Small Numbers: An Essay on the Geography of Anger.* Durham, NC: Duke University Press, 2006.

Arondekar, Anjali. "Geopolitics Alert!" *GLQ* 10, no. 2 (2004): 236–40.

Arondekar, Anjali, and Geeta Patel. "Area Impossible." *GLQ* 22, no. 2 (2016): 151–71.

Bacchetta, Paula, Sunaina Maira, and Howard Winant. *Global Raciality: Empire, Postcoloniality, Decoloniality.* New York: Routledge, 2018.

Besteman, Catherine. *Militarized Global Apartheid.* Durham NC: Duke University Press, 2020.

Carby, Hazel V. *Imperial Intimacies: A Tale of Two Islands.* London: Verso, 2019.

Clarke, Kamari Maxine, and Deborah A. Thomas, eds. *Globalization and Race: Transformations in the Cultural Production of Blackness.* Durham, NC: Duke University Press, 2006.

Coronil, Fernando. "Beyond Occidentalism: Toward Nonimperial Geohistorical Categories." *Cultural Anthropology* 11, no. 1 (1996): 51–87.

Dados, Nour, and Raewyn Connell. "The Global South." *Contexts* 11, no. 1 (2012): 12–13.

Deacon, Gregory. "Driving the Devil Out: Kenya's Born-Again Election." *Journal of Religion in Africa* 45, no. 2 (2015): 200–220.

Donovan, Kevin P., Philippe M. Frowd, and Aaron K. Martin. "Introduction: ASR Forum on Surveillance in Africa; Politics, Histories, Techniques." *African Studies Review* 59, no. 2 (2016): 31–37.

Du Bois, W. E. B. *Black Reconstruction in America, 1860–1880.* New York: Harcourt Brace, 1935.

Escobar, Arturo. *Pluriversal Politics: The Real and the Possible.* Durham, NC: Duke University Press, 2020.

Freeman, Carla. "Is Local : Global as Feminine : Masculine? Rethinking the Gender of Globalization." *Signs* 26, no. 4 (2001): 1007–37.

Ghertner, D. Asher, Hudson McFann, and Daniel M. Goldstein, eds. *Futureproof: Security Aesthetics and the Management of Life.* Durham, NC: Duke University Press, 2020.

Ghosh, Sahana. "'Everything Must Match': Detection, Deception, and Migrant Illegality in the India-Bangladesh Borderlands." *American Anthropologist* 121, no. 4 (2019): 870–83.

González, Roberto J., Hugh Gusterson, and Gustaaf Houtman, eds. *Militarization: A Reader.* Durham, NC: Duke University Press, 2019.

Gonzalez, Vernadette Vicuña. *Securing Paradise: Tourism and Militarism in Hawai'i and the Philippines*. Durham, NC: Duke University Press, 2013.

Gramsci, Antonio. *Selections from the Prison Notebooks*. Edited and translated by Quintin Hoare and Geoffrey Nowell Smith. 1971; repr., London: International, 1989.

Grewal, Inderpal. "Authoritarian Patriarchy and Its Populism." *English Studies in Africa* 63, no. 1 (2020): 179–98.

Grewal, Inderpal. *Saving the Security State: Exceptional Citizens in Twenty-First-Century America*. Durham, NC: Duke University Press, 2017.

Grewal, Inderpal. "Transnational America: Race, Gender, and Citizenship after 9/11." *Social Identities* 9, no. 4 (2003): 535–61.

Grewal, Inderpal, and Caren Kaplan. "Global Identities: Theorizing Transnational Studies of Sexuality." *GLQ* 7, no. 4 (2001): 663–79.

Grewal, Inderpal, and Caren Kaplan, eds. "Introduction: Transnational Feminist Practices and Questions of Postmodernity." In *Scattered Hegemonies: Postmodernity and Transnational Feminist Practices*, edited by Inderpal Grewal and Caren Kaplan, 1–36. Minneapolis: University of Minnesota Press, 1994.

Grewal, Zareena. *Islam Is a Foreign Country: American Muslims and the Global Crisis of Authority*. New York: New York University Press, 2013.

Ho, Engseng. *The Graves of Tarim: Genealogy and Mobility across the Indian Ocean*. Berkeley: University of California Press, 2006.

John, Mary E. *Discrepant Dislocations: Feminism, Theory, and Postcolonial Histories*. Berkeley: University of California Press, 1996.

Johnson, Sylvester A. "African Americans, the Racial State, and the Cultus of War: Sacrifice and Citizenship." *Social Text*, no. 129 (2016): 41–69.

Lorde, Audre. *Sister/Outside: Essays and Speeches*. New York: Crossing, 1984.

Lowe, Lisa. *The Intimacies of Four Continents*. Durham, NC: Duke University Press, 2015.

Loyd, Jenna M., and Alison Mountz. *Boats, Borders, and Bases: Race, the Cold War, and the Rise of Migration Detention in the United States*. Oakland: University of California Press, 2018.

Lutz, Catherine A., and Lila Abu-Lughod, eds. *Language and the Politics of Emotion*. Cambridge: Cambridge University Press, 1990.

Mahmood, Saba. "Secularism, Hermeneutics, and Empire: The Politics of Islamic Reformation." *Public Culture* 18, no. 2 (2006): 323–47.

Maira, Sunaina. *Missing: Youth, Citizenship, and Empire after 9/11*. Durham, NC: Duke University Press, 2009.

Maira, Sunaina. *The 9/11 Generation: Youth, Rights, and Solidarity in the War on Terror*. New York: New York University Press, 2016.

Massey, Doreen. *For Space*. London: Sage, 2005.

McAlister, Melani. *The Kingdom of God Has No Borders*. Oxford: Oxford University Press, 2018.

McKittrick, Katherine. *Demonic Grounds: Black Women and the Cartographies of Struggle*. Minneapolis: University of Minnesota Press, 2006.

McKittrick, Katherine. "On Plantations, Prisons, and a Black Sense of Place." *Social and Cultural Geography* 12, no. 8 (2011): 947–63.

Miller, Andrea. "Data-Driven Policing and the Colonial Database." In *Counterpoints: Bay Area Data and Stories for Resisting Displacement, 1970–2017*, edited by the Anti-eviction Mapping Project, 223–30. Oakland, CA: PM, 2020.

Moallem, Minoo. *Between Warrior Brother and Veiled Sister: Islamic Fundamentalism and the Politics of Patriarchy in Iran.* Berkeley: University of California Press, 2005.

Molina, Natalia, and Daniel Martinez Ho Sang. Introduction to *Relational Formations of Race: Theory, Method, and Practice*, edited by Natalia Molina, Daniel Martinez Ho Sang, and Ramon Gutierrez, 1–18. Oakland: University of California Press, 2019.

Mountz, Alison. "Where Asylum Seekers Wait: Feminist Counter Topographies of Sites between States." *Gender, Place, and Culture* 18, no. 3: 381–99.

Mountz, Alison, and Jennifer Hyndman. "Feminist Approaches to the Global Intimate." *WSQ* 34, nos. 1–2 (2006): 446–63.

Ndlovu-Gatsheni, Sabelo J. "Decoloniality as the Future of Africa." *History Compass* 13, no. 10 (2015): 485–96.

O'Neill, Kevin Lewis. "The Soul of Security." *Social Text*, no. 111 (2012): 21–42.

Parks, Lisa, and Caren Kaplan, eds. *Life in the Age of Drone Warfare.* Durham, NC: Duke University Press, 2017.

Perera, Suvendrini, and Sherene Razack, eds. *At the Limits of Justice: Women of Colour on Terror.* Toronto: University of Toronto Press, 2014.

Pratt, Nicola. *Embodying Geopolitics: Generations of Women's Activism in Egypt, Jordan, and Lebanon.* Oakland: University of California Press, 2020.

Puar, Jasbir K., and Amit S. Rai. "Monster, Terrorist, Fag: The War on Terrorism and the Production of Docile Patriots." *Social Text*, no. 72 (2002): 117–48.

Rana, Junaid. *Terrifying Muslims: Race and Labor in the South Asian Diaspora.* Durham, NC: Duke University Press, 2011.

Razavi, Negar. "NatSec Feminism: Women Security Experts and the Counterterror State." *Signs* 46, no. 2 (2021): 361–86.

Schrader, Stuart. *Badges without Borders: How Global Counterinsurgency Transformed American Policing.* Oakland: University of California Press, 2019.

Schober, E. *Base Encounters: US Armed Forces in South Korea.* London: Pluto, 2016.

Shohat, Ella. "Area Studies, Gender Studies, and the Cartographies of Knowledge." *Social Text*, no. 72 (2002): 67–78.

Smith, Sara. *Intimate Geopolitics: Love, Territory, and the Future on India's Northern Threshold.* New Brunswick, NJ: Rutgers University Press, 2020.

Stoler, Ann. "Colonial Toxicities in a Recursive Mode." *Postcolonial Studies* 21, no. 4: 542–47.

Tahir, Madiha. "The Containment Zone." In Parks and Kaplan, *Life in the Age of Drone Warfare*, 220–40.

Thomas, Deborah A., and Kamari Maxine Clarke. "Introduction: Globalization and the Transformation of Race." In *Globalization and Race: Transformations in the Cultural Production of Blackness*, edited by Kamari Maxine Clarke and Deborah A. Thomas, 1–37. Durham, NC: Duke University Press, 2006.

Can Black Lives Matter in a Black Country?

Deborah A. Thomas

This essay interrogates a relation. It probes the project of security (which I am defining as the protection of whiteness, class hierarchy, and heteropatriarchy) in relation to the desire for safety (which I will gloss as "having somebody"). In probing this relation within a context in which police violence and extrajudicial killing are not typically seen as part of the global phenomenon of anti-Black racism, it seeks to contribute to a conversation in which raciality is not tethered to physicality, but instead is grounded in both historical-ideological and onto-epistemological phenomena that produce whiteness as the apex of humanity in the modern West.[1] This production presumes not only transparency and universality, but also determination and causality.[2] In other words, having defined itself as universal reason and absolute perspectivity, the interior humanity against which all exterior Others are compared and measured (and found wanting), Western European empire inhabits the expression of sovereignty, not only within Europe but also throughout the postcolonial world and its diasporas.

This sovereignty is obsessed with security, which Laurence Ralph has defined as "both the nostalgic yearning for a previous era and the regulation and surveillance of bodies."[3] It is obsessed with security because its conquest, cannibalism, and disavowal of exteriority is never seamless nor complete. It is always potentially undone by that which fails to recognize it, by that which refuses it in intentional and unconscious ways. In Jamaica, these moments of refusal have been both quotidian/fleeting and transnational/durative, and these categories are themselves co-constituting.

I will proceed by exploring the relation between security and safety through the rubric of diaspora in two senses—first as a phenomenon of

Social Text 152 · Vol. 40, No. 3 · September 2022

DOI 10.1215/01642472-9771035   © 2022 Duke University Press

Western modernity via plantation-based New World slavery, which catalyzed the development of enduring categories of (non)personhood and their elaboration into hierarchies of humanity; and second as a phenomenon of migration and the constitution of transnational sociocultural spheres.[4] Diaspora, thus, generates forms of pan-Africanism and Black consciousness as much as it produces agendas related to transnational governance and global security infrastructures. I will argue that to more complexly understand security from the South, we must hold these two notions of diaspora in productive tension. This will help us to conceptualize security as a racializing project grounded in coloniality, even within majority Black spaces, and it will illuminate other terrains on which to build accountability and safety.

Moreover, in interrogating the relation between the project of security and the desire for safety, I will show that while the former is imagined and enacted transnationally and globally (but is nevertheless authorized through and in the name of the state), the latter is grounded locally and requires the intimacy of trusting relationships. Analyzing this relation within a majority Black postcolonial context allows us to more obviously reframe the problems of legitimacy and accountability outside the dialectic in which Blackness signifies a contradiction within liberal democratic humanism, and in which security is equated with peace. As Orlando Patterson has recently reminded us, it is "perhaps not an accident that democracy, in both the ancient and the modern worlds, emerged in violent ways and in the context of tremendous class and ethnic conflict."[5] Undoing this violence requires a formulation of accountability that resides outside the normative parameters of perfectible governance, and a disruption of the disavowals and deferrals that undergird imperial "Being."

Security Baselines

The answer to the question of whether Black lives matter in majority Black societies would seem, to many Americans (and especially to many African Americans), to be a given. Many would assume that because a Black country like Jamaica lacks the history of de facto apartheid that organized racial hierarchies in the United States, it would not be structured by similar racial dynamics. Such a position forgets, or disavows, that despite differences based on the particularities of time and place, white supremacy is a global phenomenon.[6] This disavowed phenomenon occasionally surfaces when we screen our film *Four Days in May* in Jamaica.[7] The film features narratives we recorded with residents of West Kingston after the "Tivoli Incursion" in 2010, when Jamaican security forces, supported by the United States, entered the Tivoli Gardens community in search of Christopher "Dudus" Coke, who had been ordered for extradition to the United

States to stand trial for gun- and drug-running charges. The search for Coke resulted in the deaths of at least seventy-four civilians. In the film, mothers describe watching their sons being executed; a brother mourns the killing of a sibling shot "execution style" next to his stepfather; an aunt talks about having to identify her nephew's body, part of which had been burned beyond recognition; other young men describe being taunted by soldiers, made to run while shots were fired after them, being tied to other men and kept in a leaky bathroom overnight, not knowing whether they were going to live or die.

Tivoli Gardens has always been what one resident called "the flagship community for the Jamaica Labour Party," the "mother" of all so-called garrison communities. Garrison communities are territorially rooted, homogenous voting neighborhoods in downtown Kingston where political support has been exchanged for contracts and other social welfare benefits, and where these exchanges are mediated through the relationship between the politician and a local "don." While the partisanship of garrison communities has been enduring, the relationship between elected politicians and community leaders became part of a more general ideological struggle during the 1970s, and transformed again as the elaboration of the transnational trades in cocaine and weapons supplanted a previously smaller-scale trafficking in ganja.[8] The latter phenomenon strengthened the role of dons vis-à-vis politicians, as dons' increasing involvement in both illicit and legitimate businesses provided politicians with financial support, in addition to the militia-like support offered during election periods.[9] Garrisons, therefore, exist as primary loci of political corruption historically and in the present. *Tivoli Gardens, downtown, garrison,* and *ghetto* mark the slot of Blackness insofar as Blackness refers to that position that both instantiates and potentially undermines and undoes the liberal order, the position that makes it insecure.

To say that geography mediates the experience of racialized abjection thus connects the question of the value of Black life to the question of security and corruption. As is also true in the United States, transformations in policing in Jamaica have typically occurred in response to instances of Black rebellion.[10] The first attempt to establish a permanent all-island police force was in 1832, the year following the general strikes organized by enslaved persons that occurred during the Christmas holidays in 1831. It was not, however, until the 1865 Morant Bay Rebellion that the Jamaica Constabulary Force (JCF) was established. During that rebellion, several hundred land-starved Black men and women marched to the courthouse to protest their excruciating economic conditions. When the governor was made aware of the march, he sent troops to hunt down the protestors; over 400 Black Jamaicans were directly killed by soldiers, an additional 350 were arrested and later executed, and hundreds more were subjected to corporal punishment. Local elected political representatives used the experience at Morant Bay to vote themselves out of direct political participation, opting instead for Crown Colony rule, a form of governance by which British territories overseas exist directly under authority of the Crown. Crown Colony rule held in Jamaica without significant constitutional change until 1944, the date that saw universal adult suffrage become law.

After Jamaica's independence from Britain in 1962, the pattern of institutionalizing security in response to Black Jamaicans' expressions of discontent continued, and an emergent concern regarding politically partisan policing deepened. In addition, the United States took on a stronger role in the development and maintenance of the local police and military forces by providing funds through the Military Assistance Program, and by training and equipping personnel through the USAID Safety Program. During the late colonial period, the United States was actively involved in funding both the Jamaica Defense Force and the Jamaica Constabulary Force, and was putting its own resources (the FBI and the CIA) in the service of surveilling groups and individuals thought to have communist leanings.

Throughout the 1960s, relations between police and politicians deteriorated, and this deterioration contributed to a high level of political violence, especially during election periods. At the time, politicians were seen as more allied to the military than to the police force, and thus, as political scientist Terry Lacey has argued, the police unleashed their dissatisfaction "not against the political masters they despised but against the 'criminal class' which certain politicians had mobilized for political warfare."[11] In other words, the police took out their own political frustrations on the downtown denizens who were being mobilized (and militarized) by political parties, not on the politicians themselves. The ultimate result of these entangled histories is that just as some Black lives seem to matter more than others, some "ghetto" lives do as well. Those living in what have been termed "garrison communities" often remain outside the realm of public empathy because they are seen to destabilize the security of democratic governance more generally. They are not always seen as worthy of protection, their deaths not always worthy of mourning.

During one postscreening discussion of our film in Kingston, a woman who had been a political representative for the People's National Party during the height of the political turf wars in the late 1970s spoke of being terrorized by the don of Tivoli Gardens during that period. She shook with rage as she asked "what Tivoli had *learned*" from their experiences in 2010. As the COVID-19 curfews wore on through May 2020, the tenth anniversary of the "Tivoli Incursion," which began on May 24, 2010, threatened to pass without remembrance. The evening of May 24 we received a phone call from a relative who works at one of the national television stations. She asked if they could show our documentary the following day, since they had neglected to organize commemorative programming related to the anniversary. As *Four Days in May* aired on Television Jamaica the evening of May 25, George Floyd was being killed by police in Minneapolis. And as Jamaicans decried this act of police violence across various media, the police and army incursion into Tivoli Gardens was rarely mentioned, generating a loud and resonant silence. "I guess people are still conflicted about Tivoli," a friend remarked.

Postcolonial Sovereignty in Jamaica

The promise of sovereignty, in British colonial contexts, has been the nominal extension of the rights of citizenship and the limited elaboration of subjectivity for those who accept a particular policing of gendered and sexual practice, on one hand, and racialized respectability on the other.[12] That the rights of this sovereignty have been rooted in practices of law and security that are also currently in flux is critical to my analysis here. Some have argued that in Jamaica, we are currently experiencing a turn toward the hegemony of a risk-oriented security strategy that is tied to agendas related to urban renewal, itself a racialized project. Central to this agenda is speculation, which requires a temporal shift toward a "future-oriented form of policing" geared toward preventing rather than solving crimes, and toward "mitigating loss over punishing wrongdoing."[13] This future orientation, like all shifts from disciplinary to biopolitical power, also diminishes the level of engagement and quality of relationship between those in authority and those in community, in part because it has been accompanied by a turn toward intensified authoritarianism and the militarization of policing through the current proliferation of states of emergency.

In 2018 in Jamaica, prolonged states of emergency came into effect in the parishes of St. James, St. Catherine, and Kingston, and by June 2020 states of emergency and zones of special operation were operative in nearly half the country's nineteen police divisions.[14] "Zones of special operation" (or ZOSOs, as they are locally termed) constitute a new legislative designation in which extreme police powers are allowed in areas where "there are reasonable grounds to believe that due to rampant criminality, gang warfare, escalating violence and murder and the threat to the rule of law and public order," normal policing is not enough.[15] A ZOSO designation lasts for an initial sixty-day period, with the possibility of extension,[16] and it is meant to entail some sort of focus on social and economic development alongside extraordinary policing. While there have been public discussions within the media about how and why ZOSOs and states of emergency now seem to regularly suspend normal police operation, thereby ultimately undermining civilian security, and while questions have been raised about how the government will transition "back" from extraordinary powers to normal policing, there is widespread popular support for these tactics in many spaces throughout Jamaica due to exhaustion and fear.[17]

The reliance on totalizing police actions like states of emergencies has also led many Jamaicans, including those in the diaspora, to question whether the government has a comprehensive crime plan. As one result of activism from the Jamaican Diaspora Foundation, among other organizations, the US Congress passed the United States–Caribbean Strategic Engagement Act of 2016 in December of that year. This law stipulates that the United States government can and should engage with governments, civil society, and the private sector throughout the Caribbean region to "reduce levels of crime and violence, curb the trafficking of illicit drugs, strengthen the rule of law, and improve citizen security." It was designed to "increase engagement with the governments of the Caribbean region, the Caribbean diaspora community in the United States, and the private sector and civil society in both the United States and the Caribbean, *and for other purposes*."[18]

Indeed, the Jamaican Diaspora Crime Intervention and Prevention Task Force (JDCIPT), part of the Jamaican Diaspora Foundation, has taken on a number of projects geared toward transnational cooperation in relation to security. They have championed cybersecurity, the development of an Intelligence Fusion Centre, a Safer Cities initiative, and youth mentorship programs. In the view that "the United States needs stronger security cooperation with the region in order to detect, deter and deny support to terrorism, terrorist activities, and encroachment by narco-terrorists into the Caribbean,"[19] the task force seeks to bring the expertise of Jamaicans living in the diaspora to bear on security issues within Jamaica.[20] Toward this end, they have conducted "fact-finding missions" during which they have met with representatives of the security forces, the state, and NGOs in Jamaica. They are also developing plans for engaged and ongoing collaboration with these groups.

Of paramount concern to the JDCIPT is corruption, and "the compelling need to create a cultural shift in police departments in the region to change from a culture of laissez-faire corruption to a culture built on values of integrity and quality service to the general public as opposed to just leadership elite."[21] Corruption was, in fact, the topic of a security roundtable the task force organized for Caribbean American Heritage Month in June 2020. During this roundtable, Trevor Munroe—director of National Integrity Action (NIA), a chapter of Transparency International—argued that because citizens don't feel their governments are doing enough to curb corruption, they no longer trust democratic institutions and are turning toward "authoritarian solutions," including militarized approaches to organized crime. Key to generating an alternative approach, Munroe stated, is building capacity within the justice sector, strengthening investigative journalism, enforcing anticorruption laws against high-level officials, and demonstrating "the impact of corruption on people's daily life" in order to get citizens involved in combating it.

We might read the efforts of the JDCIPT as an example of how transnational migrants have maintained ties to their "homelands" and, through those ties, have remained active participants in the range of discussions that affect Caribbean nationals, wherever they are living.[22] This is a view that positions diasporic Jamaicans in a helping relationship to nationals "on the rock," professionals who, because of their professed distance from the partisan corruption and political violence that compromises both security and safety in Jamaica, can offer their expertise and advice to transform the problem of crime. An alternative read would be that the Diaspora Crime Intervention and Prevention Task Force is enacting a version of what Savannah Shange has called "carceral progressivism." This is a progressivism that laments "the systemic racism of the penal system, only to call upon police as collaborators in protecting their vision of community."[23]

Within the context I am exploring here, we might interpret the JDCIPT's activism as an attempt to make both the US and Jamaican states accountable to Jamaican citizens, but without tethering this accountability to a more foundational rearrangement of the infrastructures that reproduce insecurity in the lives of poor Black Jamaicans, even as they also champion local development and mentorship initiatives. The Diaspora Foundation wants the state to work better, and they want intelligence gathering and policing to be more cooperative, efficient, and disinterested. The security they imagine does not therefore fundamentally rearrange the parameters of value placed on Black life or the normative dimensions of partisan life that continue to shape electoral politics. This is also the case when people cry out for the extraordinary measures characterized by states of emergency, ZOSOs, or other related programs; they are seeking an accountability that measures their value through the lens of the state, and that is embedded within broader patterns of corruption and clientelism. It is not insignificant that the last phrase of the summary statement of Public Law 114-291 reads, "and for other purposes." These words open a world of possibilities we cannot yet envision that might emerge in contexts we cannot yet know. The law, then, like contemporary policing, is speculative. It evokes a future anterior without a referent, and therefore indefinitely suspends the issue of accountability and its conditions of possibility. It also defers explicit discussions of state-sponsored anti-Blackness.

The Value of Black Life

Noel Chambers, a gentleman described by his niece as a "nice, strong, well-dressed Rastaman,"[24] spent forty years in a correctional facility without trial before dying at the age of eighty-one in the Tower Street Adult Correctional Centre in January 2020. He was found emaciated and covered with bedsores and bites from insects. Chambers had been charged with murder in February 1980 and was remanded into custody in 1982 but never had a trial as he had frequently, but not absolutely, been found unfit to plead. According to INDECOM, the agency that investigates allegations of abuse of the public by members of the security forces, Chambers was one of 146 mentally ill persons held by the Department of Correctional Services without trial, and one of fifteen who had been imprisoned for more than thirty years without trial.[25] This is the result of a Jamaican law maintaining that an inmate should be detained at the pleasure of the queen (during the colonial period), the governor general (during the postcolonial period), or the court (after 2007, when the Criminal Justice Administration Act was amended) if that person were unfit to plead or found guilty but suffering from a mental disorder.[26] Responding to Chambers's death, Prime Minister Andrew Holness said, "This tragedy is undoubtedly ranked amongst the most dreadful inheritances of a penal and judicial system that are in urgent need of reform."[27] And indeed, Chief Justice Bryan Sykes quickly established a Mental Health Task Force to examine the practices, policies, and procedures related to mentally ill people in custody.[28]

Chambers's sister, Joyce Davy, reported that she had advocated on his behalf for thirty years with the minister of security, with the governor general, and with various legal aid clinics. She was attempting to have him released into her custody, especially as his health began to deteriorate. She said the facility "treated him as if he didn't have anybody."[29] His case was enough of an example to George Williams, who had been arrested and charged with murder at the age of twenty in July 1970 but was deemed unfit to plead. Having spent nearly five decades in the St. Catherine Adult Correctional Centre, Williams appealed to the High Court for his release, stating, "I don't want to die like Noel Chambers."[30] The INDECOM report on Mr. Chambers's death also reported that a legal justice project had been initiated in 2017 to extricate mentally ill persons who had been incarcerated for relatively minor infractions, but that the project had stalled after having released only a handful of people. In part, this was due to the refusal of some families to accept custody of their mentally challenged relatives, and to the inability of the psychiatric hospital to accommodate them. For example, one man who had been in custody since 1977 awaiting trial on a charge of wounding could not be released because the family "hadn't forgiven him and refused to take him."[31]

On April 25, 2020, Jodian Fearon died approximately six hours after delivering a baby girl at the Spanish Town Hospital, days before her twenty-fourth birthday. A student at the University of the West Indies, Fearon had been set to deliver at St. Andrews Memorial Hospital, but they refused to admit her due to her presentation of COVID-like symptoms. Fearon had been induced because she had developed what seemed like preeclampsia, and though she had been scheduled for a cesarean section at Andrews, the team of anesthesiologists "refused to participate in the surgery."[32] Doctors attempted to transfer Fearon to the University Hospital, but that failed, and even though the Spanish Town Hospital, twenty-five kilometers away, agreed to admit her, once they arrived they were forced to wait. Complications arose during the surgery, and Fearon was then taken to the University Hospital, where she died. She later tested negative for COVID-19. After her death, a tense back-and-forth among the various institutions arose, and Fearon's family claimed that hospital administrators denied them access to her medical files. The police launched a criminal negligence probe into her death in the face of intense public outrage.

Susan Bogle, a forty-four-year-old woman living in August Town, was shot in her home by Jamaica Defence Force (JDF) soldiers who were performing police functions on Wednesday afternoon, May 27, 2020. The corporate communications unit of the police force reported that "the security forces came under heavy gunfire in the area and when the shooting subsided, a woman was seen suffering from gunshot wounds. She was taken to the hospital, where she was pronounced dead." Community residents argued, however, that the soldier ran into her house shooting behind a gunman and realized soon after that he had shot the wrong person.[33] Bogle was rushed to the University Hospital of the West Indies with her son, and was pronounced dead. An autopsy later revealed that she died of a single gunshot to the chest.

INDECOM quickly began a probe into Bogle's death, which, at the end of May, was one of 361 incidents involving police and 18 involving soldiers, the latter more than the entirety of complaints against soldiers in 2019. Bogle's death has reignited calls for "greater accountability from the security forces," and JDF Chief of Defence Staff Lieutenant General Rocky Meade reported that the JDF was in the process of testing body cameras. Minister of National Security Horace Chang reported that the police force had received more than 120 body cameras through funding from the US embassy in Jamaica, but that they were faulty and couldn't be worn with existing uniforms.[34] The minister visited August Town after Bogle's death. After walking through her home with Member of Parliament for St. Andrew Eastern Fayval Williams, the minister gave the following statement:

> In the last few weeks August Town has seen a resurfacing of major violence and I want the community to appreciate that we are not only concerned about the tragedy of Miss Bogle but we are deeply concerned about the continued level of violence, which has taken since this year, nine lives. . . . The level of violence in August Town unfortunately creates the system where this can happen. . . . When the security forces have to operate with the gunfire around them, it creates a very difficult situation for them to operate in, this can never be justified but it can be understood with what is happening here.[35]

Alexis Goffe, a restorative practices educator who is in contact with members and friends of the Bogle family, reflected with them on Minister Chang's visit to the community. They spoke about the ongoing violence they have experienced at the hands of the state and within the community itself, but they were disappointed that Minister Chang framed Susan Bogle's killing in relation to this longer history of violence. What they felt they got from Minister Chang was not a commitment to the reform of the security forces, but instead a sense that Susan Bogle's death was collateral damage in a war, unfortunate but not unexpected. In fact, at her funeral, MP Williams said, "Were it not for the violence of August Town, Susan Bogle would not have to die."

I have written about Noel Chambers, Jodian Fearon, and Susan Bogle, but I could have just as easily written about Carmichael Dawkins (a nineteen-year-old who died after a "curfew encounter" with police in Montego Bay), Tiana James (a master's student at the University of the West Indies who died after giving birth in April), or Savion Hinds (a youth killed in Stewart Town, St. Mary, by police). As far back as September 2000, researchers from Amnesty International investigated attitudes toward police in a number of urban areas, and found that "almost everyone claimed to have had direct experience of police brutality."[36] At that point, the seven-hundred-strong Jamaica Constabulary Force (JCF) had been found responsible for an average of 140 deaths per year over the previous ten years, almost five times the rate of South Africa.[37] While police reports most usually describe fatal shootings as the result of gunfire exchanges that were initiated by armed civilians, statistical evidence "shows that the number of civilians fatally shot by police is consistently many times larger than the number of police officers shot by civilians."[38] Jamaica has long had one of the highest extrajudicial killing rates in the world, and compounding this have been innumerable reports of human rights abuses and the torture of suspects while in police custody, of the covering up of evidence, and of the failure to prosecute. And as we have seen, this is only compounded by an inability to provide regular and appropriate mental health care. It might not seem surprising, within this context, that George Floyd's murder by police in Minneapolis over Memorial Day weekend would have generated intense public response across media platforms in Jamaica.

Mediating Raciality

Following the deaths of Chambers, Fearon, and Bogle, Peter Espeut, an environmentalist and columnist for the *Gleaner*, wondered whether Black lives matter in Jamaica. He gave the example of the soldiers involved in the 2010 "Tivoli Incursion" having been extended immunity from prosecution, arguing that this makes it seem acceptable for security forces to "kill in the name of the Government."[39] Daniel Thwaites, too, wondered whether Black lives matter in Jamaica. His number crunching suggests "that if the police in the US killed proportionally the same number of people as the Jamaican police, they would have killed nearly 30,000 in 2013 instead of 1,106"; that "if the US police were to kill at Jamaica's rate, during the period from 2014 to 2018 they would have killed around 65,000 more people"; and that "if Jamaicans were killed at the rate that US blacks are killed by US law enforcement, there would be about 20 such deaths annually," roughly one-seventh of those occurring in Jamaica.[40]

These commentators are pointing out that while it is important that middle- and upper-class Jamaicans recognize the ongoing travesty of police violence against African Americans, they should not turn a blind eye to this same violence occurring in Jamaica. Peter Champagnie, who had been one of the lawyers for the JDF during the West Kingston Commission of Enquiry, explicitly called out what he saw as the hypocrisy of those Jamaicans who enthusiastically followed the Black Lives Matter movement in America, but didn't know about what had happened to Noel Chambers or Susan Bogle. "The incidents of Susan Bogle and Noel Chambers," he wrote, "demonstrate in the clearest form an unwillingness to confront our own ills in society and take a proactive approach to deal with them."[41] Alfred Dawes was more scathing in his assessment. "At the risk of being branded a cynic," he wrote, "allow me to pour scorn on the ones among us with selective outrage and selective empathy for all things foreign while allowing all the worthy causes of Jamaicans suffering in an unjust system to become nine-day wonders." He continued,

> Ask yourselves, why is it that political power lies in the hands of the Black majority yet the same redlining of Black communities in the White-dominated USA exists here in Jamaica? Black communities in the US have worse schools, and education as a means to escape poverty is a dream avail-

able only to the minority. Yet after 58 years of self-rule, we have the same apartheid education system that sees poor ghetto youths stuck in crime-ridden communities because the schools they have available celebrate the student with two CSEC passes, and their address on a resume has the same effect as an African American-sounding name in America. Just as in the projects in the US, blacks in our ghettoes are at higher risk of being abused or killed by the security forces, less likely to graduate from college, less likely to get bank loans, more likely to have poorer health, and more likely to suffer from violent crime than their counterparts in non-redlined communities.[42]

Dawes is arguing that those lambasting police violence in the United States would never "go downtown and join the protests against police killings" because they learn not to "mix up" with "downtown people," they learn that "only criminals live there" and that they "are not their equals." He concludes, "Go ahead and support the Black Lives Matter movement, but suh wah, ghetto yute lives nuh matter, tuh? Where is their hashtag? When is their march?"

As a friend of mine posted on Facebook while the news of George Floyd's death was circulating, substituting "Black" for "poor" in any of the reports would reflect the ways similar conditions obtain in Jamaica. "Black" in Jamaica, remember, is often indexed through the geographical referents of "ghetto" and "downtown." This should remind us that raciality is not merely produced through the visual apprehension of familiar differences, but is built interactively, intersubjectively, and dynamically. It is felt, made, and made relevant, through relational practice with other humans, landscapes, and objects.[43] That raciality is produced relationally is also what requires an analysis that moves beyond the historical and sociological dimensions of the political economy of inequality to also parse its affective dimensions, as these are what generate performative moments of racial violence, even in majority Black settings.[44] As the editors of this issue put it, security has "multiple affective lives," and paying attention to these can help us to see both the forces that animate global imperialism and those that chip away at it.

Relation, Safety, Accountability

I want to bring us back to what Noel Chambers's sister Joyce said about her brother's condition. She said "they treated him *as if he didn't have anybody*" (emphasis mine). This speaks to the important relationship I want to parse here between safety and accountability, as to be treated like you don't have anybody is to be insecure. The security state, Achille Mbembe argues, "thrives on a *state of insecurity*," itself "a kind of passion, or rather an affect, a condition, or even a force of desire."[45] Safety, too, is a kind of passion, and a safe world is one in which people feel "connected to and cared for by others,"[46] one in which they *have somebody*, not one in which "the police keep black and other marginalized people in check through threats of arrest, incarceration, violence and death."[47] If, when people want safety, what they end up getting is security, then we need to look beyond the state for the cultivation of a different kind of accountability.

Reflecting on the deaths of Susan Bogle and Noel Chambers, Alexis Goffe stated, "I think you can have security without relationships, but you cannot have safety without relationships." And this works the other way around as well. "If you are invested in restorative practices but disconnected from relationships, it doesn't work" because there is no trust (pers. comm., June 21, 2020). In other words, to feel safe, there has to be accountability, and accountability can only be generated within the context of loving relationship. There are local models for this, models that include the practice of reasoning among Rastafari, and the community-based problem solving of groups like the Sistren Theatre Collective or the Violence Prevention Alliance. These kinds of practices do not replicate the colonial love of governance, regulation, and tutelage, but instead seek to generate mature, responsible love, "love with accountability," as Aishah Shahidah Simmons has termed it.[48]

"Love with accountability" also challenges the foundations of respectability to which postcolonial sovereignty was tethered. We see this most vividly in recent years within spheres of explicit social mobilization. Within a content in which gender-based violence is normalized and homophobia is pervasive, it is significant that new spaces are emerging through which people have come to demand accountability the forms of gender violence structuring Jamaica's infrastructural and ideological spheres. The Tambourine Army, for example, which came into being in 2017, has created platforms for women in Jamaica to publicly name those who had sexually abused or assaulted them. The explicitly public advocacy of J-FLAG (Jamaican Forum for Lesbians, All-Sexuals, and Gays, now named Equality Now), has attempted to create safe spaces for Jamaicans to participate in everyday activities that would normally render them insecure, such as publicly enjoying life as a gay family at the beach, or cheering at a track race. Other institutions like Jamaicans for Justice and the University of the West Indies Rights Advocacy Project (URAP) based at the Law School, have been supporting the rights of gay men and trans women who have been continually harassed by so-called small charges, the vagrancy and trespassing laws that have been used by police since the abolition of slavery as tools for social control and spatial exclusion. In challenging the silences that undergird public respectability, these groups are unsettling one pillar on which contemporary understandings of nationalist sovereignty stand. They are creating the conditions in which people might "have somebody," and in which their safety network is strengthened.

When the woman at our screening asked "What has Tivoli *learned* from the incursion?" she was not met with derision, even though her rage was palpable. She may not yet have been ready to do the work of account- ability herself, but the Tivoli Gardens community residents who were also at the screening did not attempt to shout her down. Instead, the woman who had identified her nephew's burned body said, "There are good and bad within Tivoli, like everywhere else." One of the youth who had described his experiences in the film stood and sincerely thanked everyone for coming, especially all the "uptown people," saying that he never would have thought so many people "cared about what happened to wi." And a longtime community activist responded gently, "I think another way to ask that question is to wonder what *Jamaica* has learned" from the incursion.

Both Chambers and our film audience were reckoning with how to generate safety from insecurity, with the cyclical quotidianity of forms of violence that comprise complex relations of scale (and our complici- ties within them), and with the ways their embodiments are marked by their geographies.[49] If, as Mbembe has argued, "the colony represents the site where sovereignty consists fundamentally in the exercise of a power outside the law,"[50] and if Blackness, in its negation of law and juridical norms, unsettles this sovereignty, then we must cultivate a sovereignty that engulfs rather than one that defers and disavows. We must also claim a form of accountability that nullifies the normative relations that uphold "Being" as the ground of subjectivity and governance. Then, Black lives might matter, in a Black country or anywhere.

Deborah A. Thomas is the R. Jean Brownlee Professor of Anthropology and the direc- tor of the Center for Experimental Ethnography at the University of Pennsylvania. She is the author of *Political Life in the Wake of the Plantation*, *Exceptional Violence*, and *Modern Blackness*, and codirector of the films *Bad Friday* and *Four Days in May*.

Notes

I am thankful to many people for help with this essay, including Tina Campt, Alexis Goffe, John L. Jackson, Jr., Laurence Ralph, Savannah Shange, and Christen Smith. I offer special gratitude also to Inderpal Grewal, Sahana Ghosh, and Samar Al- Bulushi for inviting me to participate in this special issue, and for leading the ways toward creating the kind of community of safety we all wish for, within the academy and beyond.

    1. Wynter, "Un-settling the Coloniality."
    2. Ferreira da Silva, *Toward a Global Idea of Race*; Ferreira da Silva, "1 (Life) ÷ 0 (Blackness)."
    3. Ralph, "Memory of Gold."
    4. Glick Schiller, Basch, and Szanton-Blanc, *Toward a Transnational Perspective*.
    5. Patterson, *Confounding Island*, 128; see also Mbembe, *Necropolitics*.

6. Clarke and Thomas, *Globalization and Race*; Thomas and Clarke, "Globalization and Race"; Pierre, "Slavery, Anthropological Knowledge."

7. Thomas, Wedderburn, and Bell, *Four Days in May*.

8. Sives, *Elections, Violence, and the Democratic Process*.

9. Harriott, *Understanding Crime in Jamaica*.

10. For an elaboration of these points, see Paton, "State Formation in Victorian Jamaica." In particular, Diana Paton discusses the simultaneous growth of state activity under Crown Colony rule, at the same time as populations were being denied access to the political system, and as the state was continually enhancing its capacity to suppress opposition. See also Paton, *No Bond but the Law*.

11. Lacey, *Violence and Politics in Jamaica*, 122.

12. I limn the parameters of, and current challenges to, racialized respectability elsewhere. See Thomas, *Modern Blackness*; Thomas, *Exceptional Violence*; Thomas, *Political Life*.

13. Jaffe, "Speculative Policing," 449.

14. Williams and Hyman, "JDF under Fire."

15. The Law Reform (Zones of Special Operations) (Special Security and Community Development Measures) Act, 2017, https://japarliament.gov.jm/attachments/article/339/The%20Law%20Reform%20(Zones%20of%20Special%20Operations)%20(Special%20Security%20and%20Community%20Development%20Measures)%20Act,%202017.pdf.

16. Though Minister of National Security Horace Chang announced in June 2020 that all existing zones of special operation would expire on July 25, 2020, ZOSOs were extended for ten police precincts on July 22, 2020, and most have continued to be extended since that time.

17. ZOSOs are part of a more general global trend toward police militarization, one that demonizes "'a criminal element' that pervades society and is responsible for myriad social ills," but one that ultimately also exists as "an ongoing threat to democratic stability and security" (Goldstein, "Toward a Critical Anthropology," 496). For an example of how fear and exhaustion related to criminal activity in one Brazilian *favela* led to initial support for the pacification programs in Rio, see Fahlberg, "It Was Totally Different." For an analysis of how women in Salvador, Bahia, contested both police violence and dispossession through their activism, see Perry, *Black Women*.

18. United States–Caribbean Strategic Engagement Act, Pub. L. No. 114-291 (2016), https://www.congress.gov/114/plaws/publ291/PLAW-114publ291.pdf.

19. JDCIPT, "Strategic Plan."

20. Members of the task force include Senior Intelligence Analyst Herb Nelson; Rupert Francis, professor of education and psychology; Captain Peter Whittingham, former chief of homicide with the Los Angeles Police Department; and Devon Clunis, former Winnipeg chief of police.

21. JDCIPT, "Strategic Plan."

22. For examples of this analytic direction, see Basch, Glick Schiller, and Szanton-Blanc, *Nations Unbound*; Sutton and Makiesky-Barrow, "Social Inequality"; Thomas, "Blackness across Borders."

23. Shange, *Progressive Dystopia*, 15.

24. Robinson, "'I Tried Everything.'"

25. INDECOM, the Independent Commission of Investigations, was established by an act of parliament in April 2010, and it began operation in August of that year.

26. Scott, "Courts under Fire."

27. Williams, "Tragic and Heartbreaking."

28. *Jamaica Gleaner*, "Judiciary Conducting Review."

29. Davy, quoted in Corey Robinson, "'I Tried Everything.'"

30. Williams, quoted in Barrett, "'I Don't Want to Die.'"

31. Barrett, "Justice Stalled."

32. Scott, "'Madness.'"

33. Espeut, "Do Black Lives Matter in Jamaica?"

34. Hyman, "No Eyes on Police."

35. Chang, quoted in Hyman, "Soldiers on Operation."

36. Amnesty International, *Jamaica*, 4.

37. Amnesty International, *Jamaica*, 7.

38. Amnesty International, *Jamaica*, 7.

39. Espeut, "Do Black Lives Matter in Jamaica?"

40. Thwaites, "And Then You Will See Clearly."

41. Champagnie, "Why Aren't We Confronting."

42. Dawes, "Why I Doth Not Protest Too Much."

43. M'Charek, "Beyond Fact or Fiction."

44. Achille Mbembe, in *Necropolitics*, has written about this phenomenon extensively in relation to the "African postcolony," and Christen Smith, in *Afro-Paradise*, has shown us that violence against Black bodies in Bahia was established as normative during colonial slavery, and that this was reinforced by patterns of policing that followed emancipation, through to the military dictatorship and post-1989 processes of gentrification.

45. Mbembe, *Necropolitics*, 54.

46. Stevie, "Security Does Not Mean Safety."

47. Kaba, "Yes, We Mean Literally Abolish. "

48. Simmons, *Love with Accountability.* See also Chen, Dulani, and Piepzna-Samarasinha, *Revolution Starts at Home.*

49. On complicity, see Ralph, *Torture Letters*, esp. 70–84.

50. Mbembe, "Necropolitics," 23.

References

Amnesty International. *Jamaica: Killings and Violence by Police—How Many More Victims? (Summary).* AMR 38/03/2001. 2001. https://www.amnesty.org/en/wp-content/uploads/2021/06/amr380072001en.pdf.

Barrett, Livern. "'I Don't Want to Die Like Noel Chambers'—Man in Prison for Fifty Years without Trial Pleads for Freedom." *Jamaica Gleaner*, June 17, 2020. http://jamaica-gleaner.com/article/lead-stories/20200617/i-dont-want-die-noel-chambers-man-prison-50-years-without-trial-pleads.

Barrett, Livern. "Justice Stalled—Multimillion-Dollar Project to Free Mentally Ill Inmates Fettered." *Jamaica Gleaner*, June 14, 2020. http://jamaica-gleaner.com/article/lead-stories/20200614/justice-stalled-multimillion-dollar-project-free-mentally-ill-inmates.

Basch, Linda, Nina Glick Schiller, and Cristina Szanton-Blanc. *Nations Unbound: Transnational Projects, Postcolonial Predicaments, and Deterritorialized Nation-States.* Langhorne, PA: Gordon and Breach, 1994.

Champagnie, Peter. "Why Aren't We Confronting Our Own Ills?" *Jamaica Gleaner*, June 5, 2020. http://jamaica-gleaner.com/article/letters/20200605/letter-day-why-arent-we-confronting-our-own-ills.

Chen, Ching-In, Jai Dulani, and Leah Lakshmi Piepzna-Samarasinha, eds. *The Revolution Starts at Home: Confronting Intimate Violence within Activist Communities*. Chico, CA: AK, 2011.

Clarke, M. Kamari, and Deborah A. Thomas, eds. *Globalization and Race: Transformations in the Cultural Production of Blackness*. Durham, NC: Duke University Press, 2006.

Dawes, Alfred. "Why I Doth Not Protest Too Much." *Jamaica Gleaner*, June 7, 2020. http://jamaica-gleaner.com/article/commentary/20200607/alfred-dawes-why-i-doth-not-protest-too-much.

Espeut, Peter. "Do Black Lives Matter in Jamaica?" *Jamaica Gleaner*, May 20, 2020. https://jamaica-gleaner.com/article/commentary/20200529/peter-espeut-do-black-lives-matter-jamaica.

Fahlberg, Anjuli N. "'It Was Totally Different than What We Had Before:' Perceptions of Urban Militarism under Rio de Janeiro's Pacifying Police Units." *Qualitative Sociology* 41, no. 2 (2018): 303–24.

Ferreira da Silva, Denise. "1 (Life) ÷ 0 (Blackness) = ∞ − ∞ or ∞ / ∞: On Matter beyond the Equation of Value." *e-flux*, no. 79 (2017). https://www.e-flux.com/journal/79/94686/1-life-0-blackness-or-on-matter-beyond-the-equation-of-value/.

Ferreira da Silva, Denise. *Toward a Global Idea of Race*. Minneapolis: University of Minnesota Press, 2007.

Glick Schiller, Nina, Linda Basch, and Cristina Szanton-Blanc, eds. *Toward a Transnational Perspective on Migration: Race, Class, Ethnicity, and Nationalism Reconsidered*. New York: New York Academy of Sciences, 1992.

Goldstein, Daniel. "Toward a Critical Anthropology of Security." *Current Anthropology* 51, no. 4 (2010): 487–517.

Harriott, Anthony, ed. *Understanding Crime in Jamaica: New Challenges for Public Policy*. Mona: University of the West Indies Press, 2004.

Hyman, Danae. "No Eyes on Police, Army—After Years of Promises, Not One Body Camera in Action." *Jamaica Gleaner*, June 1, 2020. http://jamaica-gleaner.com/article/lead-stories/20200601/no-eyes-police-army-after-years-promises-not-one-body-camera-action.

Hyman, Danae. "Soldiers on Operation during which Bogle Was Killed Reassigned; Weapons Confiscated." *Jamaica Gleaner*, May 31, 2020. http://jamaica-gleaner.com/article/news/20200531/soldiers-operation-during-which-bogle-was-killed-reassigned-weapons.

Jaffe, Rivke. "Speculative Policing." *Public Culture* 31, no. 3 (2019): 447–68.

Jamaica Gleaner. "Judiciary Conducting Review Arising from Noel Chambers Case." June 9, 2020. http://jamaica-gleaner.com/article/news/20200609/judiciary-conducting-review-arising-noel-chambers-case.

JDCIPT (Jamaica Diaspora Crime Intervention and Prevention Task Force). "Caribbean Community Strategic Plan for 2015–2019." JDCIPT Fact Finding Mission Report. 2019.

Kaba, Mariame. "Yes, We Mean Literally Abolish the Police." *New York Times*, June 12, 2020. http://www.nytimes.com/2020/06/12/opinion/sunday/floyd-abolish-defund-police.html.

Lacey, Terry. *Violence and Politics in Jamaica, 1960–1970: Internal Security in a Developing Country*. Totowa, NJ: Frank Cass, 1977.

Mbembe, Achille. "Necropolitics." *Public Culture* 15, no. 1 (2003): 11–40.

Mbembe, Achille. *Necropolitics*. Durham, NC: Duke University Press, 2019.

M'Charek, Amade. "Beyond Fact or Fiction: On the Materiality of Race in Practice." *Cultural Anthropology* 28, no. 3 (2013): 420–42.

Paton, Diana. *No Bond but the Law: Punishment, Race, and Gender in Jamaican State Formation, 1780–1870*. Durham, NC: Duke University Press, 2004.

Paton, Diana. "State Formation in Victorian Jamaica." In *Victorian Jamaica*, edited by Tim Barringer and Wayne Modest, 125–38. Durham, NC: Duke University Press, 2017.

Patterson, Orlando. *The Confounding Island: Jamaica and the Postcolonial Predicament*. Cambridge, MA: Belknap Press of Harvard University Press, 2019.

Perry, Keisha-Khan. *Black Women against the Land Grab: The Fight for Racial Justice in Brazil*. Minneapolis: University of Minnesota Press, 2013.

Pierre, Jemima. "Slavery, Anthropological Knowledge, and the Racialization of Africans." *Current Anthropology* 61, no. S22 (2020): S220–31.

Ralph, Laurence. "The Memory of Gold." *Transition*, no. 105 (2011): 88–105.

Ralph, Laurence. *The Torture Letters: Reckoning with Police Violence in Chicago*. Chicago: University of Chicago Press, 2020.

Robinson, Corey. "'I Tried Everything'—Sister of Man Who Died in Custody after Forty-Year Wait for Trial Speaks Out." *Jamaica Gleaner*, June 5, 2020. http://jamaica-gleaner.com/article/lead-stories/20200605/watch-i-tried-everything-sister-man-who-died-custody-after-40-year.

Scott, Romario. "Courts under Fire as Inmate Held for Forty Years Dies without Trial." *Jamaica Gleaner*, June 4, 2020. http://jamaica-gleaner.com/article/lead-stories/20200604/courts-under-fire-inmate-held-40-years-dies-without-trial.

Scott, Romario. "'Madness': Hospitals, Doctors Trade Blame as Delivering Mother Dies amid COVID Chaos." *Jamaica Gleaner*, April 27, 2020. http://jamaica-gleaner.com/article/lead-stories/20200427/madness-hospitals-doctors-trade-blame-delivering-mother-dies-amid.

Shange, Savannah. *Progressive Dystopia: Abolition, Anti-Blackness, and Schooling in San Francisco*. Durham, NC: Duke University Press, 2019.

Simmons, Aishah Shahidah. *Love with Accountability: Digging up the Roots of Childhood Sexual Abuse*. Chico, CA: AK Press, 2019.

Sives, Amanda. *Elections, Violence, and the Democratic Process in Jamaica, 1944–2007*. Kingston: Ian Randle, 2010.

Smith, Christen. *Afro-Paradise: Blackness, Violence, and Performance in Brazil*. Urbana: University of Illinois Press, 2016.

Stevie. "Security Does Not Mean Safety: #1." *Dreaming Freedom Practicing Abolition* (blog), July 19, 2019. https://abolitioniststudy.wordpress.com/2019/07/19/security-does-not-mean-safety-1/.

Sutton, Constance, and Susan Makiesky-Barrow. "Social Inequality and Sexual Status in Barbados." In *Sexual Stratification: A Cross-cultural View*, edited by Alice Schlegel, 292–325. New York: Columbia University Press, 1977.

Thomas, Deborah A. "Blackness across Borders: Jamaican Diasporas and New Politics of Citizenship." *Identities* 14, nos. 1–2 (2007): 111–33.

Thomas, Deborah A. *Exceptional Violence: Embodied Citizenship in Transnational Jamaica*. Durham, NC: Duke University Press, 2011.

Thomas, Deborah A. *Modern Blackness: Nationalism, Globalization, and the Politics of Culture in Jamaica*. Durham, NC: Duke University Press, 2004.

Thomas, Deborah A. *Political Life in the Wake of the Plantation: Sovereignty, Witnessing, Repair*. Durham, NC: Duke University Press, 2019.

Thomas, Deborah A., and Kamari M. Clarke. "Globalization and Race: Structures of Inequality, New Sovereignties, and Citizenship in a Neoliberal Era." *Annual Review of Anthropology*, no. 42 (2013): 305–25.

Thomas, Deborah A., Junior "Gabu" Wedderburn, and Deanne M. Bell, dirs. 2018. *Four Days in May: Kingston 2010*. New York: Third World Newsreel.

Thwaites, Daniel. "And Then You Will See Clearly." *Jamaica Gleaner*, June 7, 2020. https://jamaica-gleaner.com/article/commentary/20200607/daniel-thwaites-and -then-you-will-see-clearly.

Williams, Andre. "'Tragic and Heartbreaking'—PM Comments on Noel Chambers Who Died after Forty Years behind Bars without Trial." *Jamaica Gleaner*, June 6, 2020. http://jamaica-gleaner.com/article/lead-stories/20200606/tragic-and-heart breaking-pm-comments-noel-chambers-who-died-after-40.

Williams, Andre, and Danae Hyman. "JDF under Fire—Disabled Woman Killed in August Town, Complaints to INDECOM Soar." *Jamaica Gleaner*, May 28, 2020. http://jamaica-gleaner.com/article/lead-stories/20200528/jdf-under-fire-disabled -woman-killed-august-town-complaints-indecom.

Wynter, Sylvia. "Un-settling the Coloniality of Being/Power/Truth/Freedom: Towards the Human, after Man, Its Overrepresentation." In "Coloniality's Persistence," edited by Greg Thomas. Special issue, *CR: The New Centennial Review* 3, no. 3 (2003): 257–338.

From the Sky to the Streets, and Back

Geographies of Imperial Warfare in East Africa

Samar Al-Bulushi

In the 2015 thriller *Eye in the Sky*, political and military officials in the United States and United Kingdom debate whether to launch a drone strike against suspects tied to the Somalia-based al-Shabaab militant group in the Nairobi suburb of Eastleigh, a neighborhood inhabited primarily by Kenyans of Somali origin. *Eye in the Sky* depicts Eastleigh as a war-ravaged landscape entirely under the control of al-Shabaab with armed militias patrolling the streets, regulating entry and exit at makeshift checkpoints. As the film unfolds, British and American officials rely on satellite imagery to track the movements of "high-value" suspects from the Nairobi airport to a home in Eastleigh where the plan to conduct an attack is underway. While the initial objective was to capture one of the suspects, the discovery of suicide vests transforms the operational imperative from capture to kill.

Eye in the Sky features multiple war rooms: Creech Air Force Base in Las Vegas, an image analysis unit in Pearl Harbor, the British Cabinet Office Briefing Room (COBR) in Whitehall where key decision makers converge, and a military base in Sussex led by Helen Mirren as Colonel Katharine Powell. In the beginning of the film, the drone transmits images of the movement of suspected militants in Nairobi. With the help of a remote-controlled "bird" operated by a local informant played by Barkhat Abdi (famous for his role as a Somali pirate in *Captain Phillips* [dir. Paul Greengrass, 2013]), a mobile surveillance camera flutters on the outside of one home in Eastleigh, enabling visual entry through the windows. When the suspects move unexpectedly to a different home, the

Social Text 152 · Vol. 40, No. 3 · September 2022
DOI 10.1215/01642472-9771049 © 2022 Duke University Press

Figure 1. In *Eye in the Sky* (2015), Colonel Katherine Powell (played by Helen Mirren) processes the images before her from a military base in the United Kingdom: to the left is an image of the living room inside the terror suspects' home; to the right is the satellite image of the home from above.

informant manages to deploy a mobile "fly" inside of this home. Viewers are then privy to the assembly of suspected militants seated in the living room (as shown in figure 1).

The bulk of the film is devoted to the anxious dispositions of British and American military actors who fixate their gaze on a collage of video screens. Their eyes function as a weapon, as a visual register of racialization, through which Muslims are deemed to be threatening.[1] When the remote-controlled fly moves to the bedroom, the officials discover a man who is in the process of assembling suicide vests. "Shit," murmurs Colonel Powell as she processes the image before her. "This changes everything," says Lieutenant General Frank Benson (Alan Rickman). "Get legal in here right now!" Colonel Powell commands. "We need to put a hellfire through that roof!"

Despite Powell's determination to act quickly, the officials in the Cabinet Office in Whitehall become embroiled in debate about just war theory and the legality of a strike. It is with this discussion in mind that mainstream accounts of the film praise the producers for skillfully capturing the "complexities" of military decision making in the age of the drone.[2] As the characters weigh the potential risks to human life presented by a potential attack, preemption—in the form of a drone strike on the house—emerges as the preferred option. Authorization in hand, Powell and her colleagues then assume the white (wo)man's burden of preventing a seemingly imminent threat to human life in an African state that is rendered incapable of managing its own affairs.

With the onset of the war on terror, racialized visual economies about "unstable" Africa now intersect with those focused on "violent"

Islam. *Eye in the Sky* simultaneously reinforces "skepticism about Africa's ability to function" as it sets in motion Orientalist imaginative geographies of threat.[3] It is ripe for analysis about visuality and white supremacy, and about the alienation of drone optics from the people and places under surveillance and assault.[4] As a film that is almost entirely focused on the imperial war room, it is in some ways a dramatized version of the widely circulated White House Situation Room photo that centers high-level US officials as they follow live feeds of the hunt for, and assassination of, Osama bin Laden in 2011. "In this 'mesmerizing,' 'captivating' image," writes Keith Feldman, "we are asked to identify with the sovereign power of observation."[5] Whether in the form of the Situation Room image or *Eye in the Sky*, visual frames play a pivotal role in legitimating the imperial state's right to extraterritorial killing.

Rather than shift our attention to those on the receiving end of imperial violence in East Africa, I suggest that we contend with the reality that there are other war rooms—and even other "eyes in the sky."[6] While Kenya has been engaged in its own targeted operations against al-Shabaab, it is often dismissed as a proxy or mercenary force in an otherwise American-centered war. Fittingly, the Kenyan military officials depicted in the film merely follow the directives and strategic aspirations of their more powerful counterparts. *Eye in the Sky* therefore emphasizes Euro-American geographies (London, Washington, etc.) as the terrain of the political. African subjects and their geographies are either too destroyed or too subjugated to constitute the geopolitical.[7] Here we see a convergence in both popular culture and scholarly analysis, wherein Euro-American actors remain the implicit subjects of the so-called war on terror, even among critiques that are anti-imperial in ethic and orientation.[8]

Against the Eurocentric, heteronormative paradigms that continue to structure analysis of post-9/11 imperial warfare, this article asks what it would mean to decenter the view from the imperial war room.[9] What analytical openings arise when we situate empire within an expanded spatial and temporal landscape to account for the vast array of geographies and actors that have become entangled in its workings?[10] Recognizing that five African states have been drawn into a fifteen-year military occupation of Somalia, this article takes seriously the African subjects who co-constitute geographies of war making in East Africa today: the politicians who sanction the purchase of military hardware, the political and business elite who normalize militarized masculinities and femininities, the media houses that censor the brutalities of war, the logistics companies that facilitate the movement of supplies, and the troops themselves, whose morale and faith in their mission must be sustained.[11] As such, it emphasizes the mutually constitutive relationship between Black spatial knowledge and geographies of domination.[12]

Thinking at the intersection of Black geographies, subaltern studies, and transnational feminism, we have an opportunity to consider geographies of relationality across difference.[13] To speak of coconstitution and relationality is not to overlook or dismiss asymmetrical relations of power but to acknowledge that empire is sustained by and through relations with subaltern populations. This facilitates a conceptualization of the war on terror not as one single apparatus of rule, but as a series of interrelated geopolitical projects. As Madiha Tahir observes, post-9/11 US military operations in the form of drone warfare are only the most visible element of what she refers to as "distributed empire"—differentially distributed opaque networks of technologies and actors that augment the reach of the war on terror to govern more bodies and spaces.[14] This dispersal of power requires careful consideration of the geographies of militarized labor that sustain war making in Somalia, from the African Union peacekeeping mission (AMISOM) to Kenyan airstrikes against al-Shabaab.[15] By exploring the multiple geopolitical calculations that animate this "deadly dance," I direct our attention to the ways in which African geographies are not external to, but *constitutive of*, the shape-shifting formations of imperial warfare today.[16] Far from a celebration of subaltern agency, this essay engages the notion of a "subaltern geopolitics" that is mindful of asymmetries of power and that foregrounds ambiguous positions of marginality that are neither dominant nor resistant.[17] Attention to entanglement disrupts binary analytical paradigms of global/local and masculine/feminine, and calls for a deeper consideration of collaboration and complicity.

8/7 and the Geopolitics of Suspicion

On August 7, 1998, al-Qaeda militants attacked the US embassies in Nairobi and Dar es Salaam. More than two hundred Kenyans and Tanzanians were killed, in addition to twelve Americans. What transpired in the weeks and months following 8/7 was not dissimilar from what unfolded after 9/11: government officials declared "radical" Islam to be a threat, leading to mass arrests and interrogations of Muslims. Hundreds of FBI agents landed in the region, triggering the largest investigation it had ever conducted outside of US borders. Because the attacks had come on the heels of mass protests led by the Islamic Party of Kenya in the coastal city of Mombasa, Muslims on the coast were the primary targets of the investigations.[18]

The United States promptly courted the Kenyan state as a security "partner," negotiating access to Kenyan military facilities including the Port of Mombasa and airbases across central Kenya. Already a regional hub for multinational corporations and the United Nations, Kenya's position on the Indian Ocean afforded the United States unhindered access to South Asia and the Middle East. In the wake of the embarrassing exit of US forces from Somalia in 1993, Kenya's shared border with Somalia was of equal interest to American officials. The Kenyan government capitalized on this interest: at US\$88 million, it received the biggest share of President Bush's East African Counterterrorism Initiative (EACTI)—representing nearly 90 percent of the total for the region.[19] The massive influx of funds enabled the Kenyan government to create numerous domestic security bodies including the Anti-terrorism Police Unit, the Joint Terrorism Task Force, and the National Counter Terrorism Centre.[20]

While the Kenyan state was quick to align itself with the United States after 8/7, its citizens were more circumspect. Public anger directed toward al-Qaeda was paralleled by anger toward American hubris: "Why did the Americans have to bring conflict wherever they went? Why did they build their embassies in the middle of crowded cities knowing as they did of the security risks involved? Why did they appear to be more concerned with the wellbeing of their own personnel than with the hundreds of Africans killed and injured during the attack?"[21] As one Tanzanian newspaper asked, "Is America humble enough to admit that it has been wrong in its dealings with the rest of the world and that it must change in the interest of lasting peace?"[22] Despite the horrors of the attacks, Osama bin Laden soon became an icon for young people in the region, "the symbol of a counterweight to the excesses of American hegemony."[23] While the critique of US empire appealed to Christians and Muslims alike, it had particular resonance among young Muslims on the coast who increasingly linked their own experiences of surveillance and criminalization to the oppression of Muslims across the world. They took to the streets in protest not only of Kenyan antiterrorism laws and practices, but in protest of the US invasion of Afghanistan, and of ongoing injustices against Palestinians living under occupation. Looking outward across the Indian Ocean and beyond, they articulated a collective worldview that challenged dominant modes of geographic thought that privilege ideas of territory and rootedness. For Édouard Glissant, this "poetics of landscape" names other realities; the act of envisioning subaltern geographies as entwined and relational is also an act of self-assertion and humanization.[24]

It is precisely these extraterritorial imaginaries of relation that pose a threat to power. In a July 2007 report, the Combating Terrorism Center's Harmony Project at West Point argued that the presence of a "disaffected minority Muslim population" in Kenya made it an attractive place for al-Qaeda operations. The report located prospects for radicalism within the "small but significant Arab, Arab-Swahili and Somali minorities concentrated in coastal Kenya, Nairobi and several other urban centers."[25] It further pointed to Indian Ocean histories of trade, study, and intermarriage as indicative of the coastal population's nonnative roots, faulting the region's very diversity for obscuring distinctions between "foreign" and "local" Muslims: "Some of these, especially those with Arab lines of descent, maintain closer ties with their home countries. Indeed, many residents of Mombasa, Malindi and Lamu hold stronger ties with the Arabian Peninsula than with Kenya's own interior. These historical connections and the cover provided by a diverse population significantly reduce the visibility of foreign operatives."[26]

Let us return briefly to Katherine McKittrick, who highlights the ways in which practices of domination "naturalize both identity and place, repetitively spatializing where nondominant groups 'naturally' belong."[27] The language in this report illustrates how post-9/11 discourses about "security" rely on colonial-era framings of Africa "as the place of blacks where race, geography, and polity overlapped naturally."[28] Racial and territorial authenticity are conflated, such that "everything that is not black is out of place."[29] This naturalization of difference, writes McKittrick, is "bolstered by the ideological weight of transparent space, the idea that space 'just is,' and the illusion that the external world is readily knowable. . . . If *who* we see is tied up with *where* we see . . . then the placement of subaltern bodies deceptively hardens spatial binaries, in turn suggesting that some bodies belong, some bodies do not belong, and some bodies are out of place."[30] The conundrum facing security analysts at West Point is how to make sense of heterogeneity in the "land of blacks." The primary conceptual tools available to them are colonial mappings of territorialized nation-statehood that delineate between the norm and its exception, and that render transcontinental spatialities exceptional. Binary frames of "foreign/local" imply that Africa is a discrete entity isolated from the wider world, and yet it is precisely these transcontinental histories and modes of living, in all of their multiplicities, that have *made*—both materially and imaginatively—what we know of as "Africa" today.

Because the Indian Ocean brings to light such cross-regional histories, encounters, and connections, Isabel Hofmeyr points to its relevance for post-area studies. Employing the Indian Ocean as method, we become attuned not only to the layered and contradictory forms of place making and belonging, but equally to layered modes of sovereignty.[31] When applied to the ongoing war on terror, this complicates the notion that racialized ideas about Islam and Muslims have simply been imported into the Kenyan context. As mass-mediated ideas about the al-Shabaab militant permeate the Kenyan public sphere, they are entwined in imaginative political geographies that are both new and old. Omani rulers laid the groundwork for racial and ethnic divisions, in part through their sponsorship of Arab planters and Indian financiers, and through their importation of African slaves.[32] When the British established political control in 1890, they accentuated these divisions through laws and classificatory systems (native vs. nonnative) that heightened awareness of social difference.[33]

Somalis—much like Arabo-African Swahilis living along the coast—created a conundrum for colonial officials. Their historical patterns of mobility across the Red Sea and Indian Ocean contributed to hybrid identities that defied binary distinctions between native and nonnative.[34] Because the British colonial system eventually classified Arabs and Somalis as nonnative citizens alongside Europeans, it effectively blurred the boundaries between the colonizer and a minority *among* the colonized.[35] Classificatory regimes and technologies of rule have therefore accumulated over time to produce the notion of the "foreign" Arab or Somali Muslim. Alongside Hofmeyr's conceptualization of the "layered archive," a relational approach to the study of race and racialization enables us to move beyond the Black/white binary in order to consider multiple, crosscutting modes of alterity.[36]

What does it mean, then, to study the ways that race structures practices of surveillance and policing when those with the power to police are also Black?[37] As African states expand their surveillance capabilities, they build on an archive of surveillance practices that marked Blackness (and especially Blackness in particular places) as inherently suspect. The colonial-era *kipande* or special ID card, for example, prescribed limitations on the holder's movement in urban areas. In part designed to facilitate African labor mobility, it simultaneously functioned to enforce racial segregation. "The history of the *kipande*," writes Keren Weitzberg, "highlights both the centrality of Kenya to the making of global registration systems, and the need to re-center Africa within the history of racial capitalism."[38] Although Kenya's new biometric ID card (*Huduma Numba*) is not as explicitly racialized, it is informed by historical and structural processes of value differentiation that include an enduring investment in whiteness. Alongside other modes of surveillance and policing, it is a means through which difference is produced. While the specific context of the war on terror is one in which surveillance reinscribes ideas about Arab and Somali "foreigners," a singular analytic frame of xenophobia fails to account for the afterlife of colonialism, wherein whiteness as an organizing philosophy has been normalized so thoroughly "as not to need white bodies to enact it; Black bodies do the work just as effectively."[39]

Between eyes on the street, in the home, and in the sky, surveillance is productive of new structures of feeling, forms of subjectivity, and practices of citizenship.[40] Citizens under suspicion are subject to the jurisdiction of multiple sovereigns in a transnational field of power that is elusive and shape-shifting.[41] Because the enemy is ambiguously defined and conceived primarily as a phantom figure, the war on terror has sanctioned superfluous—often illegible—networks of police power that operate within and beyond the borders of the state. In this context, the citizen-suspect emerges as a gendered and racialized subject position from which everyday life is negotiated, shaped by the paranoia and uncertainty that come with subjection to these illegible powers, and by a contingent ability to become suspects without awareness or intent.[42]

Twenty-two-year-old Suleiman, whom I first met in Mombasa in 2014, was doubtful about whether they would ever escape this liminal position. He had been swept up in a police raid in 2013 and detained for several weeks; his subsequent appeal to a local human rights organization led to yet another arrest and brief detention. Since then, he has lived in constant fear of surveillance and targeted assassination at the hands of Kenya's Anti-terrorism Police Unit, notorious for disappearances and extrajudicial killings. "In Kenya, I will never be able to have a family," he said despondently. "If you criticize the government, you are branded a terrorist and they kill you." Suleiman had explored the possibility of migration to Somalia or the Middle East—*not* to join an armed group, but to escape the uncertainty of life as a citizen-suspect.

Residents of Eastleigh, too, regularly contend with the realities of life under constant suspicion. The rise in al-Shabaab attacks, coupled with the influx of Somalis into this suburb of Nairobi, has prompted anxieties about the spread of the so-called terrorist threat to the nation's capital. In this context, Somalis emerge as a threat to Kenyanness—a constructed identity that portends to be settled and devoid of ambiguity, and that disavows the historical conditions in which Somalis came to be present in Kenya.[43] As political leaders and national media outlets refer to the neighborhood as a "terrorists' haven," they shape public fears and sentiments about anyone and anything connected to Eastleigh, popularly referred to as "little Mogadishu."[44] In October 2011, for example—coinciding with the Kenyan military's invasion of Somalia—Assistant Minister for Internal Security Orwa Ojodeh compared al-Shabaab to a snake "with its tail in Somalia and its head in Eastleigh"[45] By conjuring a geography that ties Eastleigh to Somalia, Ojodeh marked Eastleigh as a key battlespace in Kenya's war against al-Shabaab.[46] The most spectacular effects of this classification unfolded in April 2014. In an operation dubbed Sanitize Eastleigh, thousands of Kenyan security personnel descended on the neighborhood, moving from house to house to identify and remove individuals suspected of ties to al-Shabaab. Over four thousand people were arrested, and at least one thousand were subsequently held in Nairobi's Kasarani stadium, with some detained for months before they were released or deported to Somalia.

Target Somalia

In June 2021, a Kenyan military airstrike in southern Somalia killed Sahra Aden and her youngest child. Sahra's husband Ali was out of the house when the warplane struck his family home in El Adde.[47] "I found my house destroyed, my wife Sahra Aden and the baby she suckled dead," said Ali. The Somali government condemned what it referred to as "indiscriminate" airstrikes, accusing the Kenyan military of operating under the guise "of carrying out operations against extremism."[48] This was not the first time the Kenyan Defence Forces (KDF) dropped a bomb on Somalia. In fact, air power has been an integral element of Operation Linda Nchi (Protect the Nation), when the Kenyan military invaded the country in October 2011.[49]

Ethiopia was the first African military to intervene in Somalia in December 2006, sending thousands of troops across the border backed by US-supplied aerial reconnaissance. At the time, the Islamic Courts Union (ICU) had presided over six months of relative stability in Somalia. Despite US government claims that the courts had ties to al-Qaeda, they were an indigenous response to CIA-backed warlords, whose drug and weapons trafficking had subjected Somalis to years of violence and uncertainty.[50] The ICU's popularity grew not because of a unified Islamist ideology, but because of a shared desire to counteract the warlords. In the wake of the invasion, most of its leadership was driven into exile, prompting more militant factions to emerge. The intervention and occupation of Somalia by foreign troops thus planted the seeds for the growth of what is now known as al-Shabaab.[51]

The first known US airstrikes in Somalia occurred in 2007 under President George W. Bush. Kenya has served as a launch pad for these strikes, with the Combined Joint Task Force–Horn of Africa (CJTF-HOA) operating from Manda Bay military base near the northeastern town of Lamu.[52] While it was under the Obama administration that US drone strikes increased significantly, President Trump signed a directive in March 2017 expanding the discretionary authority of the military to conduct airstrikes and raids in Somalia.[53] This led to a dramatic escalation in US drone strikes, contributing to approximately nine hundred to one thousand deaths between 2016 and 2019.[54]

But to focus only on the US military is to retain a limited, circumscribed view of what is in fact a more complex and entangled terrain, one that demands a more expansive conceptualization of empire. Albeit with significantly fewer resources, the Kenyan state has actively pursued its own interests, building on a long history of operating strategically in the global realm.[55] The October 2011 invasion of Somalia followed a series of smaller-scale infiltrations, relying on US-trained Ranger-style special forces.[56] Leaders in Nairobi crafted the "Jubaland policy," designed to create a buffer zone between Kenya and Somalia in the Somalia's Juba Valley.[57] Following a series of cross-border kidnappings attributed to al-Shabaab, the government invoked Article 51 of the United Nations Charter, citing the right to self-defense. On October 16, 2011, it deployed two battalions on the ground, while relying on air power composed of F-5 combat aircraft as well as MD 500 and Z-9 transport helicopters. Over the last ten years, it has continued to rely on a combination of ground and air power in Somalia. A December 2017 United Nations report, for example, alleged that Kenyan air strikes had contributed to at least forty civilian deaths in a twenty-two-month period between 2015 and 2017.[58]

Operation Linda Nchi ("Defend the Country") represented the first time in Kenyan history that its military had invaded another state. The government quickly garnered diplomatic support for its operations: in a meeting between Mwai Kibaki, Yoweri Museveni of Uganda, and Sheikh Sharif Ahmed of Somalia, the three leaders jointly characterized the Kenyan incursion as a "historic opportunity" to defeat Islamic terrorism.[59] But within a few months, Kenyan officials were forced to contend with the price of their operations—observers estimated that the deployment had cost $180 million.[60] When the African Union Peace and Security Council agreed to incorporate Kenyan troops into its peacekeeping mission (AMISOM), it both conferred legitimacy for maintaining a military presence in Somalia and deflected the costs onto the AU's international donors.[61]

Established in 2007 with authorization from the UN Security Council, AMISOM was mandated to protect the Transitional Federal Government and to restore stability to Somalia. It began as a small deployment of 1,650 troops and grew to a force of 22,000 from five African states (Burundi, Djibouti, Ethiopia, Kenya, Uganda). Moving beyond essentialized imaginings of Somalia as undifferentiated "ungoverned" space, we have an opportunity here to reflect on the microgeographies of transnational military supply chains like AMISOM, where officials employ military cartographic practices to divide the country into a series of different spaces:[62] Ugandan troops are deployed in sector 1, which comprises the regions of Banadir and Lower Shabelle. Kenyan forces are responsible for sector 2, comprising Lower and Middle Jubba. Sector 3, comprising Bay and Bakool as well as Gedo (subsector 3), comes under Ethiopian command. Djiboutian forces are in charge of sector 4, which covers Hiiraan and Galgaduud, while Burundian forces are in charge of sector 5, which covers the Middle Shabelle region.

Each of these "sectors" represent a confluence of labor, land, and capital, requiring the active or tacit collaboration of a range of actors within and beyond the borders of Somalia.[63] Attention to the built environment has the potential to reveal not simply defensive architectures, but equally the offices, housing barracks, leisure facilities, roads, and runways that are needed for everyday operations. Meanwhile, the African troops themselves remain imperceptible as social, political, and geographic subjects whose racialized labor is relevant to our understandings of the infrastructure of imperial warfare.[64] From the quotidian spatial practices of these troops (exercise routines, operating checkpoints, erecting roadblocks, etc.) we develop an understanding of the dynamic aspects of these spaces and the interactions of various actors within them. The daily affective labor of "winning hearts and minds" is in tension with the explicitly violent domain of their work: as AMISOM troops are increasingly tasked with counterinsurgency operations, relationships with the Somali population have deteriorated, leading to rising death tolls of civilians and soldiers alike. But these everyday dynamics rarely garner international attention.[65] The rhetoric of "peacekeeping" ensures that outside observers continue to conceive of AMISOM as something other than what it is: a transnational apparatus of violent labor that exploits group-differentiated vulnerability to premature death.[66]

The distribution of African troops to different regions of Somalia points to the relationship between the "who," the "where," and the "how" of imperial warfare. It is increasingly difficult to identify the "face" of empire, as more and more operations are conducted by partner forces. This requires a more complex analysis of imperial war-making in the region—both to account for the limited powers of the drone, and to grapple with the imbrication of entities like AMISOM in transnational military supply chains that reproduce racial capitalist formations. "Often hidden from view," write McKittrick and Clyde Woods, Black histories, bodies, and experiences "are implicated in the production of space."[67] This demands "an interdisciplinary understanding of space and place-making that enmeshes rather than separates, different theoretical trajectories and spatial concerns."[68] Such an approach—which recognizes that Black subjectivities operate both within and against hegemonic understandings of nation, race, place, and membership—enables us to reimagine the subject and place of the East African warscape, bringing into focus "networks and relations of power, resistance, histories, and the everyday, rather than locations that are simply subjugated, perpetually ghettoized, or ungeographic."[69] Thus we have an opportunity to consider the relational geographies that sustain imperial war-making infrastructures in Africa today.

"Kicking Ass"

News coverage of the June 2021 strike was limited in Kenya, with just one national paper picking up a report by Reuters.[70] Kenyans' responses on Twitter ranged from celebration ("We are finally kicking ass") to denial ("reckless reporting"; "That is not a Kenyan jet fighter, wtf lol fake news").[71] These responses demonstrate that Kenya's war against al-Shabaab is as much a cultural field of representation and meaning as it is a violent endeavor. In what follows, I explore the institution of the military as an important site for the production of militarized masculinity. As we shall see, religion and gender have been central to this project, and to the cultivation of ideas about just war.

In the wake of the devastating 2007–8 postelection violence that left one thousand dead and half a million displaced, the International Criminal Court issued indictments against Uhuru Kenyatta and William Ruto, accusing them of being indirect coperpetrators of the violence. At the time, the two men were campaigning for the office of the president and vice president, respectively. The indictments by a foreign, seemingly more powerful, entity risked emasculating the figure of the Kenyan leader, whose power has long centered around the phallus.[72] Redirecting the public's attention to the threat posed by an external enemy thus created an opening to remasculinize the patriarchal leader, and to unite an otherwise divided country.

War making has also become the site both for geopolitical contestations of manhood. Neighboring states like Ethiopia and Uganda, for example, were quick to perform their role as muscular warriors ready to defeat the enemy: Ethiopia was the first to invade Somalia in December 2006, and Uganda followed suit in 2007 by deploying troops to serve under the auspices of AMISOM. These militarized response by Ethiopia and Uganda triggered gendered anxieties about the Kenyan military. In September 2011, President Museveni of Uganda reportedly questioned the masculinity of the Kenyan military when he described the KDF as a "career army" that was incapable of fighting insurgents in Somalia.[73] "Is Kenya used to fighting like this (bush and guerrilla warfare)?" he asked.

Historically, Kenya has been a key contributor to UN peacekeeping efforts, but has been reluctant to dispatch troops to peace operations with an enforcement component. Its decision to join AMISOM thus represented a departure, as did the decision to launch a full-fledged invasion of Somalia. Never before had the state sent its military into sustained combat abroad. In the face of ridicule by Museveni, Kenyan commentators soon wondered aloud about what a failure to participate in the war against al-Shabaab would mean for Kenyan masculinity. One journalist derided what he characterized as "the seeming impotence of our security apparatus," arguing that the call to war "is a demonstration that a sleeping lion will only take so much provocation, and no doubt it will be a source of pride that Kenya can hit back at a bunch of extremist crazies."[74] Another declared, "There is no man like one who has taken up arms in defense of his farm, his village, and its right to chart its own destiny."[75] Highlighting the significance of gender anxieties for what he refers to as "Kenyan Politics as Male Spectacle," Keguro Macharia observed that war would function akin to Viagra. "Our boys will prove they are MEN. No. Longer. Impotent."[76]

One month after Museveni chided Kenyan masculinity, the Kenyan Defense Forces invaded Somalia. "Troops off to war," declared the *Daily Nation*.[77] Social and national media outlets were soon flooded with images of proud men in uniform, and with patriotic declarations about Kenyan troops as national heroes. Since that time, in a marked shift from his predecessors, the president has appeared in military uniform on numerous occasions, arguing that he wants to build unity and support for Kenyan soldiers who have sacrificed on behalf of the nation.

The war on terror has provided a platform for the ruling class to simultaneously distract from the state's own complicity in patterns of interethnic and electoral violence at home, and to cultivate what Catherine Lutz refers to as the "military normal."[78] On the one-year anniversary of the invasion at the first annual "Kenya Defense Forces Day," Kenyans were invited to publicly express their support for soldiers fighting on the frontline. In these spaces, militarism, masculinity, and sacrificial citizenship are conjoined, with Kenyan troops emerging as the exemplary national hero. The annual National Prayer Breakfast and *Mashjuaa* (Heroes) Day offer supplementary venues for Kenyans to recognize the ultimate sacrifice: fighting and dying for the nation in a war against "the very epitome of evil."[79] The subtext of state rhetoric about sacrifice is that an explicitly Christian morality guides its actions against al-Shabaab. Everyday politics both feed into and reflect a Christian majority sensibility that has increasingly assumed a Pentecostal, evangelical tone.[80] Because the military's role in Somalia is primarily framed in the language of peacekeeping, Kenyans are encouraged to perceive their troops as Black knights—heroes who have sacrificed their lives for the greater good.[81]

Ultimately, however, this peacekeeper masculinity is not far removed from idealized notions of the brave, heroic warrior. In a two-page spread published in a Christmas weekend edition of the *Daily Nation* in 2019, readers learned of the "untold story" of the Kenyan military's war against al-Shabaab, replete with images that provided a "front seat view of the battles our gallant soldiers have fought and the sacrifices they have made."[82] Describing an operation that took place seven years prior in the Somali port city of Kismayu, the newspaper recounted the heroic story of Major Douglas Bulukhu, who led a team of elite soldiers in a mission to quell a group of al-Shabaab militants on the "most dangerous beach on earth." The paper's dramatic rendering of this operation was a plug for a newly released book published by the Kenyan military that highlights the growth of the Kenyan Army from a "single infantry battalion to a modern mission-capable force." The book, titled *The Soldier's Legacy*, is the second to be published by the military detailing the valiant role of its forces in the war against al-Shabaab.[83]

Kenyan women are increasingly invited to assume stereotypically masculine roles. Uhuru Kenyatta has expressed his support for gender integration and equitable participation in the Kenyan military, "hitherto largely a masculine domain."[84] Seemingly benign gendered policy frameworks constitute a form of "embedded feminism" whereby feminist discourse is invoked to consolidate militarism and counterterrorism.[85] In August 2019, Kenya inaugurated its first elite all-female Special Weapons and Tactics (SWAT) team trained to thwart terror threats. As the state seizes every opportunity to perform its cosmopolitan brand of militarism, we learn that female fighter pilots, too, "rule the skies." These realities— that Kenya conducts its own aerial operations against al-Shabaab—and that women are just as likely to pull the trigger—complicate the racialized, gendered, and scalar enactments of power from above that are traditionally associated with white/male/global. They unfix African geographies from their "natural" place seemingly outside of and disconnected from the geopolitical and provide spatial clues about the coconstitution of imperial warfare.

The Lenana Road Liberals

In April 2015, roughly one week after the al-Shabaab attacks on Garissa University College in northeastern Kenya, I participated in a small gathering of approximately ten prominent actors in Nairobi to discuss what had transpired in Garissa. In attendance was a member of Parliament representing northeastern Kenya and a range of Kenyan NGO leaders. The participants in the room maintain professional, and in some cases, social relationships with top officials in President Uhuru Kenyatta's cabinet, and with leaders in the diplomatic community. By this, I mean that they constitute members of the ruling class, and interact with some of the most powerful actors in Kenya in closed-door meetings, embassy compounds, malls, and cafés.

We were gathered in the offices of an NGO that is housed in a high-rise building in the middle-class neighborhood of Kilimani, where many of the city's largest NGOs are headquartered. Like many of the surrounding buildings, the gated compound and high-rise complex insulate its working professionals (referred to by one of my interlocutors as "the Lenana Road liberals")[86] from the surrounding city. At a time when terrorist attacks compounded already existing anxieties about urban crime, the gathering place offered a vertical cocoon, a comfortable distancing from the uncertainties below.[87] As we sat together around one large table, the ensuing discussion shed light on the subaltern ruling-class sensibilities of security that structure and facilitate imperial warfare. Focused primarily on the failures of the Kenyan security apparatus, my fellow attendees sought to understand how the Garissa University attack had occurred in spite of the Kenyan state's substantial investment in enhancing its security infrastructure. For the actors around the table, the violence that unfolded in Garissa was the product of dysfunction—of a breakdown of order. "Are they incompetent?" one participant asked in reference to the security apparatus. "Do they care? Why is Kenya so vulnerable? We have the capacity to monitor phone calls, our intelligence systems could have prevented this, so what is going on here? Do we have to become autocratic to be effective?"

Eventually, we moved to discuss strategy. The focus shifted to a citizen-centered approach to security, or what one participant referred to as "cultural vigilance." "What can we do to be prepared for the next attack?" she asked. "How can our spaces like malls and schools be better equipped with emergency procedures and contingency plans? What can we learn from other countries?" The "cultural vigilance" that this participant referred to meant working closely with the business community to ensure that malls set up fire drills and detailed escape routes. It meant working with the Kenyan government to develop a "national response." And it meant turning to the UK and US governments to learn about their use of air marshals and surveillance cameras as deterrents. The inclination was for more policing rather than less, and for policing to be dispersed to multiple actors. Their own sense of precarity worked to rescale the spatiality of violence and threat, and to rationalize the militarization of urban space.[88]

As this gathering illustrates, Kenyans are not simply bystanders who happen to be inadvertently caught up in the politics of a seemingly external, "global" project of endless war. Much like the troops serving on the frontlines, the African managerial class remains largely imperceptible in existing analysis of imperial warfare on the continent, despite their various roles sanctioning the purchase of military hardware, authorizing expansive forms of surveillance and policing, and attaching symbolism to the figure of the soldier-hero. These actors' imbrication in global war making disrupts linear frames, pointing instead to geographies of interrelation.

We have a growing understanding of the US military footprint in the region, from drone bases to cooperative security locations led by the US Africa Command (AFRICOM).[89] Yet an exclusive focus on AFRICOM is to maintain a unidimensional conceptualization of necro- and geopolitics. It is to uphold hegemonic knowledge systems that center whiteness as the terrain of the geopolitical. In these knowledge systems, Africa and Africans— whether the AMISOM troops who police the streets of Somalia, the Kenyan fighter pilots who "rule the skies," or the Lenana Road liberals who plan fire drills and escape routes—remain objects in place, disconnected from the production of power and space. Their own entanglement in the geopolitical remains outside the frame, seemingly illegible as worldmaking practice. Our challenge is to bring into focus these sites and those who inhabit them in order to grapple with the diffuse set of actors that coconstitute imperial warfare in East Africa today.

Samar Al-Bulushi is assistant professor of anthropology at the University of California, Irvine. Her published work has appeared in *American Anthropologist*, *Cultural Dynamics*, and *Security Dialogue*, and she has written for public outlets including *Africa Is a Country*, *Jacobin*, and *Warscapes*.

Notes

I am exceptionally grateful for the engaged feedback I received on early drafts of this article from the anonymous reviewers, and from Sahana Ghosh, Inderpal Grewal, Madiha Tahir, Negar Razavi, Kristin Peterson, and Hannah Appel. I also received helpful comments from participants at the workshop on Religion, Gender, and the Politics of Security at Yale University in April 2019. Special thanks to my coeditors Sahana Ghosh and Inderpal Grewal, and to Jayna Brown and Marie Buck at *Social Text*.

1. Virilio, *War and Cinema*; Feldman, "Empire's Verticality."

2. See, e.g., Lawson, "Eye in the Sky."

3. Grovogui, "Come to Africa," 428. On imaginative geographies, see Said, *Orientalism*; Gregory, *Colonial Present*.

4. Visuality has been an integral instrument of power, from the slave plantation to the war on terror. See Browne, *Dark Matters*; Mirzoeff, *Right to Look*.

5. Feldman, "Empire's Verticality," 336.

6. Engseng Ho sought to explore the view from the imperial ship "as seen from a smaller boat sailing the same seas." Here, I am curious about the view from other war rooms. See Ho, "Empire through Diasporic Eyes."

7. McKittrick, "On Plantations."

8. For more on the intellectual Eurocentrism underpinning scholarship on security and imperial intervention, see Sabaratnam, "Avatars of Eurocentrism."

9. Jasbir Puar observes that heteronormative penetration paradigms continue to inform feminist theorizations of global conquest and war. See Puar, *Terrorist Assemblages*.

10. See Coronil, "After Empire."

11. McKittrick and Woods, "No One Knows."

12. McKittrick, *Demonic Grounds*.

13. I join others in highlighting the potential for cross-fertilization between Black geographies and African geographies. Alex Weheliye notes the oft forgotten significance of the Algerian war of liberation for dismantling Western thought. Although the Black radical tradition is mainly invoked in diasporic spaces, Wangui Kimari and Henrik Ernston observe that there is much to be gained in "letting it return to Africa." See Weheliye, *Habeas Viscus*; Kimari and Ernston, "Imperial Remains"; Pierre, *Predicaments of Blackness*; Daley and Murrey, "Defiant Scholarship."

14. Tahir, "Grounding Drone Warfare."

15. For more on the global army that supports imperial warfare, see Moore, "Empire's Labor."

16. See Gregory, "Dirty Dancing," 30. As Katherine McKittrick notes, the margin is part of the story, not the end of the story. McKittrick, *Demonic Grounds*, 134.

17. Sharp, "Subaltern Geopolitics." Donald Moore reminds us that Antonio Gramsci's conceptualization of subalternity is one that emphasizes relationality and embeddedness within multiple fields of power. Moore, "Subaltern Struggles and the Politics of Place."

18. Prestholdt, "Kenya, the United States, and Counterterrorism."

19. Omeje, "War on Terror."

20. Bachmann, "Kenya and International Security."

21. Devji, *Landscapes of the Jihad*, x–xi. Families of the Kenyan and Tanzanian victims confronted the unspoken hierarchies in the US government's valuation of human lives, as the compensation offered to them paled in comparison to what was offered to their American counterparts.

22. See Sharp, "Subaltern Geopolitics."

23. Prestholdt, "Superpower Osama," 323.

24. Glissant, *Poetics of Relation*.

25. Brown, Shapiro, and Watts, "Al-Qaida's (Mis)adventures."

26. Brown, Shapiro, and Watts, "Al-Qaida's (Mis)adventures," 51.

27. McKittrick, *Demonic Grounds*, xv.

28. Akyeampong, "Race, Identity, and Citizenship," 299.

29. Mbembe, "African Modes of Self-Writing," 256. See also Mbembe, *Critique of Black Reason*.

30. McKittrick, *Demonic Grounds*, xv.

31. Hofmeyr, "Complicating Sea."

32. Glassman, "Slower than a Massacre."

33. Mamdani, *Citizen and Subject*. As other scholars have observed, however, modes of self-identification in everyday life have always been fluid—with racial identities and meanings shifting according to context. See Brennan, *Taifa*.

34. Weitzberg, *We Do Not Have Borders*; Prestholdt, "Politics of the Soil."

35. Mamdani, "Beyond Settler and Native."

36. S. Al-Bulushi, "Race, Space, and Terror."

37. See, also, Thomas, "Can Black Lives Matter in a Black Country?"

38. Weitzberg, "Biometrics, Race Making, and White Exceptionalism," 41.

39. Mungai, "Whiteness Conference." See also Y. Al-Bulushi, "Global Threat."

40. In February 2016, Kenya purchased a Boeing-manufactured ScanEagle drone from the US to conduct aerial surveillance within Kenyan territory. Business Daily Africa, "Kenya Buys Sh1bn Pilotless Aircraft in War on Al Shabaab."

41. See, also, Ghosh "Living through Surveillance."

42. S. Al-Bulushi, "Citizen-Suspect."

43. Rinelli and Opondo, "Affective Economies."

44. Koross, "How Eastleigh Turned into a Terrorist Haven."

45. Quist-Arcton, "Tensions Run High in Kenya's Little Mogadishu."

46. Rinelli and Opondo, "Affective Economies."

47. Reuters, "Kenyan Air Strike in Somalia."

48. Garowe Online, "KDF Condemned of Killing Innocent Civilians in Somalia Airstrikes."

49. Chau, "Linda Nchi from the Sky?"

50. Scahill, *Dirty Wars*.

51. See Elmi, "Revisiting United States Policy"; Scahill, *Dirty Wars*; Besteman, "Experimenting in Somalia."

52. Barnett, "Americans Have Landed." The United States has also relied on its military base in Djibouti for operations in Somalia.

53. The US military launched more drone strikes in Somalia in the first four months of 2020 than it did during Barack Obama's eight-year term in office. See Turse, "U.S. Airstrikes Hit All-Time High."

54. Sperber, "'Collateral Damage' of the U.S.'s Unofficial War in Somalia."

55. Makinda, "Quiet Diplomacy"; Branch, *Kenya*.

56. Anderson and McKnight, "Kenya at War."

57. Some have noted the economic motivations underlying the Jubaland policy, observing the significance of the LAPSSET (Lamu Port Southern Sudan Ethiopia Transport Corridor) project for linking the northeastern part of the country with the oilfields in Southern Sudan, as well as with more than eighty million people in the Ethiopian market.

58. Office of the High Commission for Human Rights, "Protection of Civilians."

59. Chonghaile, "Somalia, Kenya and Uganda Pledge to Defeat Al-Shabaab." On a trip to Israel in November 2011, then Prime Minister Raila Odinga met with Benjamin Netanyahu, who promised to help Kenya "rid its territory of fundamentalist elements." See *BBC News*, "Israel-Kenya Deal."

60. Throup, "Kenya's Intervention."

61. Williams, "Joining AMISOM."

62. Higate and Henry, "Space, Performance, and Everyday Security."

63. See also Lutz, "Bases, Empire, and Global Response."

64. Here I am indebted to McKittrick's discussion of Ralph Ellison's *Invisible Man*. See McKittrick, *Demonic Grounds*.

65. It is estimated that AMISOM fatalities ranged from 1,483 to 1,884 for the period between March 2007 and December 2018. See Williams, "Update."

66. Here I am employing Ruth Wilson Gilmore's definition of racism. Gilmore, *Golden Gulag*, 28.

67. McKittrick and Woods, "No One Knows," 4.

68. McKittrick and Woods, "No One Knows," 7.

69. McKittrick and Woods, "No One Knows," 7. See also Hawthorne, "Black Matters."

70. Reuters, "Kenyan Air Strike."

71. Wambua, "We are finally kicking ass"; Wambui K., "Reckless reporting from standard."

72. See Musila, "Phallocracies and Gynocratic Transgressions."

73. *Daily Monitor*, "Wikileaks: Museveni Discredits Kenya Army."

74. Gaitho, "Kenya's Foray against Al-Shabaab Will Not Be Easy but It Is Necessary."

75. Mathiu, "Kenya Has No Choice on the Matter of Al-Shabaab."

76. Macharia, "War as Viagla."

77. Ngirachu, "Kenya: Troops Off to War."

78. Lutz, "Military Normal."

79. Migue and Oloch, *Operation Linda Nchi*.

80. Deacon and Lynch, "Allowing Satan In?"

81. The term *black knight* is a twist on the title of Sherene Razack's book *Dark Threats, White Knights*.

82. Gisesa, "The Untold Story of KDF War against Al-Shabaab Fighters."

83. See also Migue and Oloch, *Operation Linda Nchi*.

84. Ministry of Defense, "Message from his Excellency the President."

85. On embedded feminism, see Hunt, "'Embedded Feminism.'" See also Grewal, "Saving the Security State"; Nesiah, "Feminism as Counter-terrorism."

86. For more on gated compounds in Kenya, see Gluck, "Security Urbanism"; Goodman, "'Going Vertical.'"

87. On the notion of a vertical cocoon, see Graham, *Vertical.*

88. See esp. Aas, "(In)Security-at-a-Distance"; Graham, "Cities under Siege." It is in this sense that Nairobi's Westgate Mall was characterized as a "war zone" during the three-day standoff with al-Shabaab in September 2013, when full-fledged war had been ongoing in Somalia since 2006 in the wake of the Kenyan and Ethiopian invasions.

89. Moore and Walker, "Tracing the US Military's Presence."

References

Aas, Katja Franko. "(In)Security-at-a-Distance: Rescaling Justice, Risk, and Warfare in a Transnational Age." *Global Crime* 13, no. 4 (2012): 235–53.

Akyeampong, Emmanuel K. "Race, Identity, and Citizenship in Black Africa : The Case of the Lebanese in Ghana." *Journal of the International African Institute* 76, no. 3 (2006): 297–323.

Al-Bulushi, Samar. "Citizen-Suspect: Navigating Surveillance and Policing in Urban Kenya." *American Anthropologist* 123, no. 4 (2021): 1–14.

Al-Bulushi, Samar. "Race, Space, and 'Terror': Notes from East Africa." *Security Dialogue* 52, no. S (2021): 115–23.

Al-Bulushi, Yousuf. "The Global Threat of Race in the Decomposition of Struggle." *Safundi* 21, no. 2 (2020): 140–65.

Anderson, D. M., and J. McKnight. "Kenya at War: Al-Shabaab and Its Enemies in Eastern Africa." *African Affairs*, no. 454 (2014): 1–27.

Bachmann, Jan. "Kenya and International Security: Enabling Globalisation, Stabilising 'Stateness,' and Deploying Enforcement." *Globalizations* 9, no. 1 (2012): 125–43.

Barnett, Thomas. "The Americans Have Landed." *Esquire*, July 2007. https://classic .esquire.com/article/2007/7/1/the-americans-have-landed.

BBC News. "Israel-Kenya Deal to Help Fight Somalia's Al-Shabab." November 14, 2011. https://www.bbc.com/news/world-africa-15725632.

Besteman, Catherine. "Experimenting in Somalia: The New Security Empire." *Anthropological Theory* 17, no. 3 (2017): 404–20.

Branch, Daniel. *Kenya: Between Hope and Despair, 1963–2011.* New Haven, CT: Yale University Press, 2011.

Brennan, James R. *Taifa: Making Nation and Race in Urban Tanzania.* Athens: Ohio University Press, 2012.

Brown, Vahid, Jacob N. Shapiro, and Clinton Watts. "Al-Qaida's (Mis)Adventures in the Horn of Africa." West Point, NY: Harmony Project, Combating Terrorism Center at West Point, 2007. https://ctc.usma.edu/al-qaidas-misadventures -in-the-horn-of-africa/.

Browne, Simone. *Dark Matters: On the Surveillance of Blackness.* Durham, NC: Duke University Press, 2015.

Business Daily Africa. "Kenya Buys Sh1bn Pilotless Aircraft in War on Al Shabaab." February 24, 2016. https://www.businessdailyafrica.com/bd/economy/kenya-buys -sh1bn-pilotless-aircraft-in-war-on-al-shabaab-2109296.

Chau, Donovan C. "Linda Nchi from the Sky? Kenyan Air Counterinsurgency Operations in Somalia." *Comparative Strategy* 37, no. 3 (2018): 220–34.

Chonghaile, Clar Ni. "Somalia, Kenya and Uganda Pledge to Defeat Al-Shabaab." *Guardian*, November 17, 2011. https://www.theguardian.com/world/2011/nov/17 somalia-kenya-al-shabaab-uganda.

Coronil, Fernando. "After Empire: Reflections on Imperialism from the Americas." In *Imperial Formations*, edited by Ann Laura Stoler, Carole McGranahan, and Peter C. Perdue, 241–71. Santa Fe, NM: School for Advanced Research Press, 2007.

Daily Monitor. "Wikileaks: Museveni Discredits Kenya Army." September 9, 2011. https://www.monitor.co.ug/uganda/news/national/wikileaks-museveni-discredits -kenya-army-1499718.

Daley, Patricia O., and Amber Murrey. "Defiant Scholarship: Dismantling Coloniality in Contemporary African Geographies." *Singapore Journal of Tropical Geography*, 43, no. 2 (2022): 1–18.

Deacon, Gregory, and Gabrielle Lynch. "Allowing Satan In? Moving toward a Political Economy of Neo-Pentecostalism in Kenya." *Journal of Religion in Africa* 43, no. 2 (2013): 108–30.

Devji, Faisal. *Landscapes of the Jihad: Militancy, Morality, Modernity.* Ithaca, NY: Cornell University Press, 2005.

Duncanson, Claire. "Forces for Good? Narratives of Military Masculinity in Peace-Keeping Operations." *International Feminist Journal of Politics* 11, no. 1 (2009): 63–80.

Elmi, Afyare Abdi. "Revisiting United States Policy Toward Somalia." In *Securing Africa*, edited by Malinda S. Smith, 173–92. New York: Routledge, 2010.

Feldman, Keith P. "Empire's Verticality: The Af/Pak Frontier, Visual Culture, and Racialization from Above." *Comparative American Studies* 9, no. 4 (2011): 325–41.

Gaitho, Macharia. "Kenya's Foray against Al-Shabaab Will Not Be Easy, but It Is Necessary." *Daily Nation*, October 17, 2011. https://nation.africa/kenya/blogs -opinion/blogs/macharia-gaitho/kenya-s-foray-against-al-shabaab-will-not-be -easy-but-it-is-necessary--787090.

Garowe Online. "KDF Condemned of Killing Innocent Civilians in Somalia Airstrikes." June 5, 2021. https://www.garoweonline.com/en/news/somalia/kdf-condemned -of-killing-innocent-civilians-in-somalia-airstrikes.

Ghosh, Sahana. "Living through Surveillance: Recasting the Study of Civil and Military Relations." *Comparative Studies of South Asia, Africa and the Middle East* 39, no. 3 (2019): 421–24.

Gilmore, Ruth Wilson. *Golden Gulag: Prisons, Surplus, and Opposition in Globalizing California.* Berkeley: University of California Press, 2007.

Gisesa, Nyambega. "The Untold Story of KDF War against Al-Shabaab Fighters." *Daily Nation*, December 20, 2019. https://nation.africa/kenya/news/the -untold-story-of-kdf-war-against-al-shabaab-fighters-234602.

Glassman, Jonathon. "Slower than a Massacre: The Multiple Sources of Racial Thought in Colonial Africa." *American Historical Review* 109, no. 3 (2004): 720–54.

Glissant, Édouard. *Poetics of Relation.* Ann Arbor: University of Michigan Press, 1997.

Gluck, Zoltan. "Security Urbanism and the Counterterror State in Kenya." *Anthropological Theory* 17, no. 3 (2107): 297–321.

Goodman, Zoë. "'Going Vertical' in Times of Insecurity: Constructing Proximity and Distance through a Kenyan Gated High-Rise." *Focaal*, no. 86 (2020): 24–35.

Graham, Stephen. *Cities under Siege: The New Military Urbanism*. New York: Verso, 2010.

Graham, Stephen. *Vertical: The City from Satellites to Bunkers*. New York: Verso, 2018.

Gregory, Derek. *The Colonial Present: Afghanistan, Palestine, Iraq*. Malden, MA: Wiley-Blackwell, 2004.

Gregory, Derek. "Dirty Dancing." In *Life in the Age of Drone Warfare*, edited by Lisa Parks and Caren Kaplan, 25–58. Durham, NC: Duke University Press, 2017.

Grewal, Inderpal. *Saving the Security State: Exceptional Citizens in Twenty-First-Century America*. Durham, NC: Duke University Press, 2017.

Grovogui, Siba N. "Come to Africa: A Hermeneutics of Race in International Theory." *Alternatives: Global, Local, Political* 26, no. 4 (2001): 425–48.

Hawthorne, Camilla. "Black Matters Are Spatial Matters: Black Geographies for the Twenty-First Century." *Geography Compass* 13, no. 11 (2019): 1–13.

Higate, Paul, and Marsha Henry. "Space, Performance, and Everyday Security in the Peacekeeping Context." *International Peacekeeping* 17, no. 1 (2010): 32–48.

Ho, Engseng. "Empire through Diasporic Eyes: A View from the Other Boat." *Comparative Studies in Society and History* 46, no. 2 (2004): 210–46.

Hofmeyr, Isabel. "The Complicating Sea: The Indian Ocean as Method." *Comparative Studies of South Asia, Africa and the Middle East* 32, no. 3 (2012): 584–90.

Hood, Gavin, dir. 2016. *Eye in the Sky*. Toronto: Entertainment One.

Hunt, Krista. "'Embedded Feminism' and the War on Terror." In *(En)Gendering the War on Terror: War Stories and Camouflaged Politics*, edited by Kim Rygiel and Krista Hunt, 51–71. Farnham, UK: Ashgate, 2006.

Kimari, Wangui, and Henrik Ernstson. "Imperial Remains and Imperial Invitations: Centering Race within the Contemporary Large-Scale Infrastructures of East Africa." *Antipode* 52, no. 3 (2020): 825–46.

Koross, Kibwott. "How Eastleigh Turned into a Terrorist Haven." *Standard*. April 5, 2014. https://www.standardmedia.co.ke/nairobi/article/2000108637/how-eastleigh-turned-into-a-terrorists-haven.

Lawson, Ewan. "Eye in the Sky." *RUSI Journal* 161, no. 3 (2016): 74–76.

Lutz, Catherine. "Bases, Empire, and Global Response." In *The Bases of Empire: The Global Struggle against U.S. Military Posts*, edited by Catherine Lutz, 1–46. New York: New York University Press, 2009.

Lutz, Catherine. "The Military Normal: Feeling at Home with Counterinsurgency in the United States." In *The Counter-Counterinsurgency Manual; or, Notes on Demilitarizing American Society*, by Network of Concerned Anthropologists, 23–37. Chicago: Prickly Paradigm, 2009.

Macharia, Keguro. "War as Viagla." *Gukira* (blog), October 21, 2011. https://gukira.wordpress.com/2011/10/21/war-as-viagla/.

Makinda, S. M. "From Quiet Diplomacy to Cold War Politics: Kenya's Foreign Policy." *Third World Quarterly* 5, no. 2 (1983): 300–319.

Mamdani, Mahmood. "Beyond Settler and Native as Political Identities: Overcoming the Political Legacy of Colonialism." *Comparative Studies in Society and History* 43, no. 4 (2001): 651–64.

Mathiu, "Kenya Has No Choice on the Matter of Al-Shabaab." *Daily Nation*, October 20, 2011. https://www.nation.co.ke/kenya/blogs-opinion/blogs/mutuma-mathiu/kenya-has-no-choice-on-this-matter-of-al-shabaab-the-war-must-go-on-787454.

Mbembe, Achille. "African Modes of Self-Writing." *Public Culture* 14, no. 1 (2002): 239–73.

Mbembe, Achille. *Critique of Black Reason*. Durham, NC: Duke University Press, 2017.

McKittrick, Katherine. *Demonic Grounds: Black Women and the Cartographies of Struggle*. Minneapolis: University of Minnesota Press, 2006.

McKittrick, Katherine. "On Plantations, Prisons, and a Black Sense of Place." *Social and Cultural Geography* 12, no. 8 (2011): 947–63.

McKittrick, Katherine, and Clyde Woods. "No One Knows the Mysteries at the Bottom of the Ocean." In *Black Geographies and the Politics of Place*, edited by Katherine McKittrick and Clyde Woods, 1–13. Boston: South End, 2007.

Migue, Pius, and Oscar Oluoch. *Operation Linda Nchi: Kenya's Military Experience in Somalia*. Nairobi: Ministry of Defense, 2014.

Ministry of Defense. "Message from his Excellency the President." *Republic of Kenya Ministry of Defense Gender Policy*, May 2017. https://zdoc.pub/republic-of-kenya -ministry-of-defence-gender-policy.html.

Mirzoeff, Nicholas. *The Right to Look: A Counterhistory of Visuality*. Durham, NC: Duke University Press, 2011.

Moore, Adam. *Empire's Labor: The Global Army That Supports US Wars*. Ithaca, NY: Cornell University Press, 2019.

Moore, Adam, and James Walker. "Tracing the US Military's Presence in Africa." *Geopolitics* 21, no. 3 (2016): 686–716.

Moore, Donald S. "Subaltern Struggles and the Politics of Place: Remapping Resistance in Zimbabwe's Eastern Highlands." *Cultural Anthropology* 13, no. 3 (1998): 344–81.

Mungai, Christine. "The Whiteness Conference." *Adi Magazine*, no. 6 (2021). https:// adimagazine.com/articles/whiteness-conference/.

Musila, Grace. "Phallocracies and Gynocratic Transgressions: Gender, State Power, and Kenyan Public Life." *Africa Insight* 39, no. 1 (2009): 39–57.

Nesiah, Vasuki. "Feminism as Counter-terrorism: The Seduction of Power." In *Gender, National Security, and Counter-terrorism: Human Rights Perspectives*, edited by Jane Huckerby and Margaret Satterthwaite, 127–51. New York: Routledge, 2013.

Ngirachu, John. "Kenya: Troops Off to War," *Daily Nation*, October 15, 2011. https:// allafrica.com/stories/201110160138.html.

Office of the High Commission for Human Rights. "Protection of Civilians: Building the Foundation for Peace, Security, and Human Rights." December 2017. https:// www.ohchr.org/sites/default/files/Documents/Countries/SO/ReportProtection ofCivilians.pdf.

Omeje, Kenneth. "The War on Terror and the Crisis of Postcoloniality in Africa." *African Journal of International Affairs* 11, no. 2 (2008): 89–114.

Pierre, Jemima. *The Predicament of Blackness: Postcolonial Ghana and the Politics of Race*. Chicago: University of Chicago Press, 2013.

Prestholdt, Jeremy. "Kenya, the United States, and Counterterrorism." *Africa Today* 57, no. 4 (2011): 2–27.

Prestholdt, Jeremy. "Politics of the Soil: Separatism, Autochthony, and Decolonization at the Kenyan Coast." *Journal of African History* 55, no. 2 (2014): 249–70.

Prestholdt, Jeremy. "Superpower Osama." In *Making a World after Empire: The Bandung Moment and Its Political Afterlives*, edited by Christopher J. Lee, 315–50. Athens: Ohio University Press, 2010.

Puar, Jasbir K. *Terrorist Assemblages: Homonationalism in Queer Times*. Durham, NC: Duke University Press, 2007.

Quist-Arcton, Ofeibea. "Tensions Run High in Kenya's Little Mogadishu." *NPR*,

November 18, 2011. https://www.npr.org/2011/11/19/142530740/tension-runs-high-in-kenyas-little-mogadishu.

Razack, Sherene H. *Dark Threats, White Knights: The Somalia Affair, Peacekeeping, and the New Imperialism.* Toronto: University of Toronto Press, 2004.

Reuters. "Kenyan Air Strike in Somalia Allegedly Kills Woman and Her Child." *Standard* (Nairobi), June 8, 2021. https://www.standardmedia.co.ke/world/article/2001415115/kenyan-air-strike-in-somalia-allegedly-kills-woman-and-her-child.

Rinelli, Lorenzo, and Sam Okoth Opondo. "Affective Economies: Eastleigh's Metalogistics, Urban Anxieties, and the Mapping of Diasporic City Life." *African and Black Diaspora* 6, no. 2 (2013): 236–50.

Sabaratnam, Meera. "Avatars of Eurocentrism in the Critique of the Liberal Peace." *Security Dialogue* 44, no. 3 (2013): 259–78.

Said, Edward. *Orientalism.* New York: Pantheon, 1978.

Scahill, Jeremy. *Dirty Wars: The World Is a Battlefield.* New York: Nation, 2013.

Sharp, Joanne. "Subaltern Geopolitics." *Geoforum* 42, no. 3 (2011): 271–73.

Sperber, Amanda. "'The Collateral Damage' of the U.S.'s Unofficial War in Somalia." *In These Times*, December 16, 2019. https://inthesetimes.com/features/us-air-strikes-somalia-al-shabab-ISIS-pentagon-civilian-casualties.html.

Tahir, Madiha. *Grounding Drone Warfare: Imperial Entanglements, Technopolitics, and Ghostly States in the Tribal Areas, Pakistan.* PhD diss., Columbia University, 2020.

Thomas, Deborah. "Can Black Lives Matter in a Black Country" *Social Text*, no. 152 (2022): 17–35.

Throup, David W. "Kenya's Intervention in Somalia." Center for Strategic and International Studies, February 6, 2012. https://www.csis.org/analysis/kenya's-intervention-somalia.

Turse, Nick. "U.S. Airstrikes Hit All-Time High as Coronovirus Spreads in Somalia." *Intercept*, April 22, 2020. https://theintercept.com/2020/04/22/coronavirus-somalia-airstrikes/.

Virilio, Paul. *War and Cinema: The Logistics of Perception.* London: Verso, 1989.

Wambua, Dennis K. (@Dennis_Kyallo1). "We are finally kicking ass." Twitter, June 8, 2021, 2:25 p.m. https://twitter.com/Dennis_Kyallo1/status/1402376354998501379.

Wambui K. (@regina_isaack). "Reckless reporting from standard." Twitter, June 8, 2021, 2:38 a.m. https://twitter.com/regina_isaack/status/1402198229379432449.

Weheliye, Alexander G. *Habeas Viscus: Racializing Assemblages, Biopolitics, and Black Feminist Theories of the Human.* Durham, NC: Duke University Press, 2014.

Weitzberg, Keren. "Biometrics, Race Making, and White Exceptionalism: The Controversy over Universal Fingerprinting in Kenya." *Journal of African History* 61, no. 1 (2020): 23–43.

Weitzberg, Keren. *We Do Not Have Borders: Greater Somalia and the Predicaments of Belonging in Kenya.* Athens: Ohio University Press, 2017.

Williams, Paul D. "Joining AMISOM: Why Six African States Contributed Troops to the African Union Mission in Somalia." *Journal of Eastern African Studies* 12, no. 1 (2018): 172–92.

Williams, Paul D. "An Update on How Many Fatalities AMISOM Has Suffered." *IPI Global Observatory*, September 10, 2019. https://theglobalobservatory.org/2019/09/update-how-many-fatalities-amisom-has-suffered/.

Domestic Affairs

National Security and the Politics of Protest at India's "Friendly" Borderlands

Sahana Ghosh

What acts, attentions, and affects in sites of national security comprise protest where, it is said, there is no place for it? How are protests and security regimes related over the question of difference? In India, a denial of protest by the security state can come, simply put, in the form either of violent repression, as abundantly displayed in its frontiers from Kashmir to Manipur, or as an insistence on peace, a peace ostensibly so democratic that obviates the need for protest. In this essay, I invite you to think with and from this latter position. The opening questions frame my exploration of the religious and gendered logics through which the Indian security state manages dissent and difference and reinforces its sovereignty as a liberal democracy. This reinforcement hinges on interlinked inclusions and exclusions across a variegated national security geography. My focus is on the agrarian borderlands in the eastern state of West Bengal, within which falls more than half of India's 4,096-kilometer-long border with Bangladesh, and that have been the locus of increasingly militarized border security in recent decades.[1] I will argue that the security regime of the postcolonial Indian state relies on heteropatriarchal gender norms and the discourse of the family to produce unequal minority citizens and secure their subordinated inclusion, while concealing the terms of this relation of power as such. Reading protests otherwise turns up some cracks in this story.

I take sites of national security to mean both specific places and generic spaces (e.g., borderlands, Maoist-controlled areas) that have been deemed as sensitive and in need of securitization. By the state's own logic, the national security importance of such places and spaces is reflected in their militarization, with the expectation that society and economy in

Social Text 152 · Vol. 40, No. 3 · September 2022
DOI 10.1215/01642472-9771063 © 2022 Duke University Press

such sites must be reorganized to prioritize security infrastructure and practices. However, the security state has many faces and while security infrastructures—that is, the armed forces, intelligence agencies, and juridical structures—are shared across the national security geography, the tactics and discourses deployed are highly varied. In focusing on a borderland, I am also broadly interested in examining the affective work of security regimes at and through borders.

One morning in September 2015, a hundred-odd residents, primarily Bengali Muslim, blocked a road that connected villages and two Border Security Force (BSF) outposts along India's eastern border with Bangladesh in the district of Coochbehar, West Bengal.[2] A college-going Muslim student from one of these border villages had been beaten up by the BSF on this route the previous day, and enraged residents put up a blockade at that particular checkpoint in protest. India has been fencing its side of the winding border with Bangladesh since the late 1980s and increasing its security presence in the borderlands to preempt and intercept illegal crossings of people and goods.[3] Not only does a steel and barbed wire fence now cut through agrarian fields and rural settlements adjacent to the 4,096-kilometer-long border, Indian borderland residents, who are predominantly Muslim, tribal, and depressed caste, are subject to ever more security and surveillance practices.[4] Moreover, in the Hindutva imaginary, this border is being simplified as a religious border keeping Hindu territory and demography secure from its Muslim neighbors. How does such a simplified equation between religion and security play out for the security state's rule in the borderlands? For the everyday life of national security in borderlands is a tautology: you need militarized security because borderlands are suspicious spaces of clandestine crossings and where "illegal immigrants" may be detected;[5] crossings are clandestine, risky, and profitable with more and more border security. National security in the borderlands means that residents have to live with and navigate intense border security and surveillance in their daily lives. This was one of innumerable incidents where borderland residents were harassed, detained, and physically injured by the BSF, they claimed, and this blockade was to demand specific and broad changes in Indian border security practices. "We are Indian citizens, why are we being humiliated?" they asked.[6]

To address such a question in the space of this tautology, is to cause a ripple. The blockade drew senior officers out of the BSF's urban headquarters to the borderland checkpoint and into an open dialogue with the protesters. After a couple hours of

> *kotha-barta* (Bengali)
>> *baat-cheet* (Hindi)
>>> dialogue (English word, used frequently in Bengali and Hindi speech)

Figure 1. Young men looking at the pictured report of the protest (inset) in the days after. Photograph by the author, September 2015.

in the sweltering afternoon sun and across the fault lines of translation between Hindi and Bengali, the matter was declared resolved. The BSF had agreed to meet some demands and take some others to higher authorities; men and women were satisfied that the state officials had listened to them in person and finally engaged their claims. They shared their points of view with a local journalist who had arrived to cover the protest only to find that it was nearly over. Even as the air turned from tense to jubilant, some of the leading protesters cautioned that they would continue their movement (*andolon*) if the promises made were broken. The journalist noted down the facts of the matter for a report that would read something like this. Then the leaders posed for the journalist's camera (see fig. 1) and agreed that this "friendly border" was no place for violence. The protesters dispersed and before long the fallow field on which strident footsteps had brought so many bodies together was empty again.

The blockade was over.

But for many weeks, discussions about the *dialogue* reverberated through teashops and kitchens and around dusty checkpoints, anxious Bengali speech licking around the English word. I watched as residents, especially enraged young men, returned repeatedly to the text and image in the local newspaper reporting this protest (fig. 1). Poring over the poor-quality picture of the "dialogue," the smiles of participants seemed fainter still as they struggled to see in that representation the rage and humiliation that had lit a fire in them, had driven them to block the road and confront the Indian security state.

A week later, when I brought up this blockade with a BSF officer at a neighboring outpost, he dismissed it, saying, "Look here, this is a peaceful place, this is a *friendly border*. There should be no such protest/trouble (*harkat*) here. This is no Kashmir or Northeast."[7] The Indian and Bangladeshi states officially maintain that this is a "friendly" border in contradistinction to the region's more volatile and hostile India-Pakistan border. The officer's verdict on the truth of this place hinges on this distinguishing friendliness. Well, then, had the protest succeeded or had it failed? Who had listened and who had the last word? And most importantly, what did the assertion of a "friendly border" mean in relation to discontent and political action? In a world where protests have become such mediatized events that oftentimes the very goal of protests is to attract media attention to an issue,[8] this blockade was highly local. I follow scholars who have called for a critical engagement with place and locality especially in attending to political subjectivity and expressions of political protest.[9] Despite its limited circulation,[10] these questions stubbornly lingered.

If the sounds, sites, and signs of protest reveal much about the injustices they name and contest, how might we read this "small voice"[11] of protest, to paraphrase subaltern studies historian Ranajit Guha, otherwise?

Affections and Disaffections

Protests against the security state are particularly rich sites to grasp fissures, fictions, and structuring frames: protests not only contest dominant state narratives about risk and national security, they illuminate experiences of marginalization and exclusion. However, as transnational feminist scholars Elena Cohen, Melissa Forbis, and Deepti Misri remind us, *what counts as protest* is an equally critical question so that originary sites, notions of agency, and modes of action are not reified.[12] In that spirit, the pages that follow hover in the space of doubt created by some stubborn, unresolved questions—Is it over? Did it succeed? What was heard and what remains?—about the life of the protest. In becoming a protest, collective action can present visions of democratic politics that are sometimes difficult to see and hear through the fog of liberalism. Indeed, articulation of action *as* protest can itself push the bounds of permissible politics.

Political and juridical naming produces spaces and actors. This has been most lethally evident in recent years in South Asia as exclusionary definitions of the national, nationalism, and national security have become hegemonic across the region. The "troubled" peripheries of northeastern India, the burning and raging of Kashmir's "paradise" to be set free by forcible inclusion in the Indian republic, and the "porous" border with Bangladesh through which cattle and illegal immigrants flow, are but a few examples of such phrases that name political conditions in the Indian popular imaginary.[13] These prefixes are not simply descriptive in their valence but highly polemical in the versions of history and politics they present. Their usage foretells certain forms of politics—including affective ones—and forecloses others. To examine, then, how affections and disaffections are constructed, enforced, and policed in hegemonic nationalist terms, is to cast a comparative eye across a geography of protest where some are met with tear gas, some with deliberate shooting to maim, while some are steadfastly unheard.[14] Furthermore, *how* a space is located within the national security geography—friendly, troubled, disturbed—is predicated on and calls forth profoundly gendered and racialized relations of power by which minority citizens are defined, accommodated, or erased. I raise this comparative frame not to suggest equivalence but to underline, as a recent transnational feminist statement has, this connected history and geography of violence as foundational to nation-state-making in postcolonial South Asia.[15] The gendered and racialized logics of national security as the organizing principle for the Indian state in contemporary times must be gleaned from this much broader regional genealogy. This specific locus, I suggest, is instructive for the logic of contradistinction as a mode of security rule more widely.

India's eastern border was first drawn with East Pakistan at the Partition of the subcontinent in 1947. Unlike in the West, where the violence of Partition primarily concentrated in massive displacements of people in just a few months before the border was closed completely, in the East, bordering unfolded through a variety of mobilities and attempts to govern them over several decades.[16] With the independence of Bangladesh through the Liberation War and redrawing of the border in 1971, the dichotomy of the hostility of the India-Pakistan border and friendliness of the India-Bangladesh one solidified in South Asian public and political discourse. In subsequent decades, the foundational tenet of India-Bangladesh friendship has been tested as India has steadily militarized its side of the border with bipartisan political support domestically. A humanitarian concern for refugees has been steadily replaced by a xenophobic and Islamophobic discourse against the "Bangladeshi infiltrator"[17] that sanctions the criminalization of borderlands as spaces of clandestine mobility and dovetails conveniently with global master narratives on terrorism.[18] The affective work of the border regime's "friendliness" must be situated in this political history as it sediments in the lives of Muslim and Rajbangsi borderland residents.

With the national dominance of militant and right-wing Hindu nationalism, Muslims in India have been violently targeted under the Modi government.[19] As terrorists in Kashmir, as cattle smugglers and beef eaters in lynchings and vigilante attacks across northern India, and as illegal immigrants in the eastern states of West Bengal and Assam: these are the prominent frames through which Muslims have been subject to hate crimes and excluded from citizenship in a nation being remade as a Hindu homeland. There is a broad genealogy of the postcolonial state's social contract with its minority citizens, ranging from the constitutional promise of secularism to the myth of the Muslim invader used by the Hindu right to present India as a *historically* Hindu nation.[20] In each instance of minoritization through which the Indian postcolonial state constitutes its dangerous populations beyond constitutional secularism, gender, religion, and race articulate together. This points us not only to the heterogeneity within the Other but more importantly, for the purpose of this essay, the work necessary to manage difference in each case. That is, border residents in eastern India, predominantly Muslim or depressed-caste Hindu, are minority citizens, but we cannot assume we know the political-emotional terms, grounded in gendered and racialized logics, by which they are rendered suspect, subordinated, and othered from fulsome democratic rights and citizenship. The intersection of gender and religious identity is not a "dimension" of security regimes but must be seen as foundational to its constitution and legitimacy. As such, *how* gender and religious identity articulate in each site and instance of the national security regime is vital to the understanding of its meanings and ends.

Emotions have been richly studied, especially by feminist and postcolonial scholars, in relation to gender, nationalism, and state making as a site of public attachments as well as exclusions.[21] Exploring the ongoing civil war between Maoist guerrillas and the Indian security state, Nandini Sundar asks, "How are emotions mobilized, conscripted and engendered during the course of civil war? In what language do states and rebels portray emotion, especially outrage?"[22] She argues that the state too vies for emotional attention in the public sphere and it is this "emotion management," that is the focus of her analysis.[23] I join Sundar and other scholars like Laleh Khalili who have turned to the role of emotions—outrage and happiness, respectively—in counterinsurgencies waged by liberal democracies, to scrutinize the role that "emotion management" plays in the security state's arsenal.[24] While this scholarship looks at the ways in which states deploy and manage emotion to shore up public legitimacy, I am interested in the "emotional management" that takes place in and about sites of national security such as borders where the state and targeted communities reckon with each other's frames of reference. Affect is sticky, writes Sara Ahmed. Elaborating on the idea of "affective economies" she argues that instead of residing in things or people, it gains currency and power from its circulations and attachments.[25] Following her, I explore the affective economy of friendliness—what makes it stick, how it circulates (or not), what work it does. However, in taking friendliness to be a *particular* affective economy of security regimes, I am also interested in its fissures and tensions: what happens when its normative politics and emotions are challenged, circulations obstructed, and alternative emotional claims foregrounded. I use the ethnographic details of a protest and its resultant turbulence to think through these questions.

Outing Humiliation under the Sun

It was words that had gotten Hasan Ali slaps and blows. A farmer woman who had been crossing the BSF checkpoint at the same time as Hasan Ali said that when the soldiers were interrogating him, after frisking and checking his identity documents, he had asked why. Everyone knew Hasan Ali, the student who had been beaten up by the BSF, since he was one of the first from his border village to go to college. The collective refrain surged: as it is, they humiliate us every day; we are poor and poorly educated. And Muslim, I added mentally, in a borderland where Bengali Muslims are especially policed and surveilled as "illegal immigrants."[26] Even our educated children get no respect, seethed Hasan Ali's parents and neighbors that evening, expressing the collective political aspiration of fulsome citizenship invested in the dignity of an educated offspring.

Hasan sat slumped over a plastic chair in the corner of the room, his bruises on display, his well-spoken confidence shaken. Word spread through neighboring villages, and people stopped by on their way to and from the bazaar. Hasan's humiliation was the spark that lit the fire. Humiliation that had gathered and sedimented in their toiling peasant bodies, frisked and pushed on their daily paths around their homes and fields, surveilled and suspected of being smugglers and criminals, insulted for being Muslims and having ties across the border in neighboring Bangladeshi villages. *Jobab chai*, we want an answer, why was he beaten? We want the soldier punished, the murmurs spread through the unlit night.

Memories of beatings, blows, insults to men and to women, to elderly and to children were relived and shared all night, I was told, gathering force like a monsoon rainstorm. The next morning without much coordination or forethought, residents of these border villages, still without paved roads, electricity, primary health, and educational facilities, rushed toward the checkpoint at which Hasan Ali had been beaten (see fig. 2). Many later told me that they were not sure what was going to happen; all they knew was that answers were being demanded. Through numerous conversations I could see that the idea of spontaneous combustion spread as fast as the details of this particular instance.[27] For once the BSF would have to come to them; their bodies would not move until the soldiers came under their scrutiny. They were going to hold up the BSF's—and all other local—passage on this rural thoroughfare.

Unlike marches or demonstrations that occur outside governmen-

Figure 2. Enraged women rushing to join the protest alongside scores of men.
Photograph by the author, September 2015.

tal offices—a readily legible and visible template of protest—this blockade and the questions staked at the checkpoint "reconfigure the materiality of public space" anew.[28] The very rubric of friendliness that allows
the security state to claim that these borderlands are peaceful places of
no conflict—where everyday movements and life are unhindered by the
work of national security, where curfewed nights are normal and necessary to protect the nation and the people—was at stake. Not only has the
policing of everyday movements of people and goods in these borderlands
with the stated aim of intercepting criminal mobilities increased in recent
years, such policing relies on gendering and sexualizing certain bodies as
risky.[29] This border security regime is hegemonic and its rationale widely
normalized. The affective economy of friendliness by which a thoroughly
ambivalent cooperation is held in fragile balance has come to be internal-
ized and expected by all.

Hasan's beating, and the blockade it sparked, was a rupture to this
fragile balance and the fictions of friendliness. Humiliation clarified people's ambivalence toward the affective demands of the border security
regime. By holding up traffic at the BSF checkpoint, residents reoccu-
pied the space as their *lived* space, seizing momentarily the power to control mobility. Men and women, recounting together their experiences past

Figure 3. BSF officers in uniform seated on chairs, Hasan Ali crouching at the center though kneeling on the ground. Photograph by the author, September 2015.

beyond differences of gender and religion, turned this gathering into an "embodied archive,"[30] ephemeral yet, of humiliation and agitation.

You can imagine that the news of an angry Muslim crowd close to the international border did not take long to travel to higher authorities. Soon the wail of sirens atop the jeeps and a cloud of dust heralded the speedy arrival of BSF officers previously unseen. The atmosphere heaved with anger but was also edged with palpable excitement. As if by historical muscle memory the villagers seated themselves on the ground, around the chairs that had materialized to seat the uniformed officers and political leaders. At last they were under the same scorching sun. We are here to listen to you, let's talk, the men in uniform and on the chairs said (see fig. 3).

But they began by talking, that too in Hindi which few Bengali rural folks understood. I stepped forward from the crowd and offered to translate. In his speech the officer acknowledged that residents suffered disruptions in their daily lives and livelihoods because of "national security" (*desh ka suraksha*) and because this was a "*friendly border*," civil-military relations had to be good and cooperative. Having framed the suffering of borderland citizens as to be expected and indeed necessary for the greater good of national security, the officer directly addressed the matter of the soldier's outburst.

Figure 4. An organizer of the protest confronting the officers and their explanations.
Photograph by the author, September 2015.

He said, "Please forgive him; that fellow was in an angry mood (*gusse me*) as he had had a bad fight with his wife on the phone just before his duty shift started. You know how it is—sometimes when you have a bad day at work you go home and take it out on your wife. Here this became reversed! He took out his anger with his wife on you!"

My translation tumbled out to an impatient crowd and at the punch line, intended to defuse the tension with a casual touch of lightness, a roar of indignation went through the group (see fig. 4). One of the young male organizers of the protest jumped up and shouted at me, "Are we their wife at home that they should take out their anger on us? Ask him." I made eye contact with some of the women seated toward the back; they rolled their eyes and rose. Perhaps they were going to leave; they had heard enough. Heated exchanges continued with outraged residents raising numerous grievances that had been simmering for a long time. After a few hours of what the security state insistently referred to as a "dialogue," the agitating residents were assured that such "excesses" would not recur and several of their functional demands would be seriously considered. It looked like the *bandh* would soon be over.

Residents of this region are Bengali Muslims and Rajbangshi Hindus, a scheduled caste in India. Muslims are roughly 14.2 percent of the population of India. Alongside "scheduled castes" and "scheduled tribes," bureaucratic terms for depressed-caste and tribal peoples, Muslims are considerably more deprived in comparison to other religious communities in the country.[31] Despite cultural heterogeneity, a majority of Indian Muslims are lower and lower middle class, constituting a "periphery within a periphery" of the working class across agrarian and urban spheres.[32] It is in this larger and longer regional context that the particularity of humiliation as experience and protest at this friendly border assumes significance. Political theorist Gopal Guru in his interventions on humiliation emphasizes two key elements as it comes to be enunciated as a political and epistemic category: the comparison of experiences across contexts and the emergence of the language of rights.[33] Political and cultural theorists of humiliation have argued that to own humiliation is to "stake a claim"[34] and that "it naturally involves the capacity to protest."[35] Reading the humiliation foregrounded in this instance in these terms enables us to view it not simply as the disempowering consequence of a violent security regime but as a form of political action and epistemological critique. This becomes especially crucial in such instances where collective action is neither mediatized as event nor legible in terms of regnant national and transnational frames.[36] The burden on the protesters is not only to articulate their accumulated injuries but to retain the ability to name and circulate their agitated gestures and emotions *within* the affective economy of friendliness. The question of making humiliation circulate as political currency and critique when the phenomenon of humiliation is rationalized and indeed reproduced by hegemonic "institutional and moral means" is to pose a radical epistemological challenge.

Let us consider for a moment what is wrong with the explanation of the soldier's anger, offered as conciliation and not offense. Framing the soldier's anger as a man's commonplace and unremarkable emotion directed toward his wife, only concedes the misdirection of anger. The implicit suggestion is that there is an acceptable level of suffering—note how the issue of regular intrusive violence is erased—that befits the friendliness and amity of this site of national security. The gendered analogy used in this explanation is not incidental nor exceptional. Rather, it surfaces the displays of power that is typically invisible and unspoken—like a gendered violence performed routinely—and actively obscured by the affective economy of friendliness. There is a candor to this confession that reveals the extent to which security regimes not only rely on displays of power but conceal them as such. Moments such as these in which the heteropatriarchal logics that naturalize arrangements of power are visible as such are thus both profoundly humiliating from the targeted community *and* potentially destabilizing for the security regime's affective economy. The misogynistic humor presumes sympathy and chauvinistic camaraderie from its audience: a man-to-man joke that simultaneously hinges on feminizing and domesticating the subjugated community. Furthermore, in constructing the perpetrator of violence as the real victim, it enacts another instance of humiliation. This is the humiliation of disqualification; you cannot even be a legitimate protester.

The Trouble with Sympathy

What does the official "friendly border" label mean to borderland residents? No matter the inconveniences and disruptions in daily itineraries that security checks had introduced into their agrarian lives and livelihoods, men, women, and children typically go about their way silently, affecting docility so as to draw as little attention as possible from the uniformed and armed soldiers. The discourse of friendliness is not all a facade, an official smokescreen imposed solely from above. Indeed, as BSF soldiers spend six-hour shifts on patrols and at semipermanent checkpoints along paths of the border villages and on the black-tarred road that runs alongside the barbed wire fence, they live and work alongside men and women working their fields, grazing animals, and walking these paths. In what I have elsewhere called "security socialities," civil-military encounters in these borderlands are indeed embedded in a range of hetero- and homosocial relations through which BSF soldiers are read and established as brothers, fathers, lovers, and sons, far away from their own families.[37] Instances of aggression—a slap here, an unfair detention there, casteist, anti-Muslim, and gendered insults galore—are punctuations in daily and lengthy proximities of conversation and engagement. The trouble with sympathy is that it is hard to escape, when invoked in such heteropatriarchal terms. So, when in the "dialogue," the officers alarmed by the rejection of their blunt defense of the soldier's errant anger and desperate to control the situation, a plea was made for good old sympathy, no one was really surprised.

Holding up his hand to the group, the same officer pointed to his fingers and renewed his conciliatory efforts. "Are all the fingers the same on one hand? No, right? Not everyone is equal in the same family (*parivar*). Every family has a black sheep. If one of our sons does something wrong, what can we do? We have to teach him, explain to him, but we cannot just throw him out, can we? We have to accept him and live with him. Otherwise the peace of the family will be broken, all families would fall apart." The crowd was hushed; there was no ready retort. The blockade was definitely over; this was the moment in which the local journalist arrived.

The security state resorts to the language of heteropatriarchal kinship and marshals the semiotic appeal of the nation as a big family. In acceding to its imperfections, the security state cast its institutional avatar in the image of another dominant normative institution, the patriarchal family. It was with this unquestionable reasoning that the gathered protesters were finally calmed down. This is not an isolated instance. Rather, it is a window into the supple language of paternalism and masculine protection, deployed by soldiers and border citizens to their own ends. For the moment, the *bandh* was over (or had failed, depending on who you asked), and a "dialogue" had resolved the matter suitably. The short-lived and eventually pacified anger of a mother or wife at a son's misdemeanor, on the other hand, can be voiced, heard, and eventually silenced for the greater good of the national family. Sympathy for soldiers performed as emotional labor for national security's sake thus constitutes Muslim border residents as emotive citizens, albeit in a limited capacity, to be included in the national *we*. Protests, then, compel us to ask, in Mel Chen's words, "How to locate and value disruption, especially when that disruption is a violation of a racial-gendered script of embodiment and movement?"[38] Protests such as these are critical not only in how they (re)direct the course of these particular events and their narratives but because they reveal the structuring work of the affective economy of friendliness within which speaking and hearing positions become intelligible such that, for a flickering moment, doubt holds radical potential.

The Indian security state's "emotional management" in these borderlands, with a predominantly Muslim demographic, takes a form that is distinct from its counterinsurgency avatar, be that in the Maoist heartlands or separatist Kashmir and the northeastern states. In each of those cases, the construction of radical alterity establishes the Kashmiri body, the Maoist body, and the tribal insurgent body to be beyond rescue and reform.[39] Affirmed as "killable," at each instance the body-collective becomes a site to dramatize/reproduce "the sovereign power of the Indian state," argues Ather Zia with regard to India's occupation of Kashmir. She notes that such lives and deaths are especially vital in "keeping intact the body of the Indian nation."[40] The management of the protest is clearly an instance for the sovereign power of the state as patriarch and the body of the nation as heteropatriarchal family to be dramatized, exemplified, and thereby reproduced. However, friendliness in the eastern borderlands portends engagement, and the subject of engagement is deemed to be both teachable and worthy of inclusion, albeit on subordinated terms. Side-stepping the question of equality in inclusion—"Are we not citizens?" as the collective question echoed, insisting on the language of citizenship instead of kinship—the state's emotional management here is to make friendliness stick. Holding up "dialogue" as an end, not a means, it seeks to transform the alienation of a community from the national body politic into a disciplined inclusion premised on the recognition of its *proper* victims and heroes and the domestic order of power. Pratiksha Baxi, in her chilling account of rape trials in India, elaborates on the "annihilating violence" masked by the socio-legal notion and technique of compromise. She writes, "Far from being an expression of collective consensus, compromise is predatory to claims of justice, and shadowed by violence or its threat. The normalizing function of the socio-legal category of compromise makes terror look like a social bargain."[41] Here I want to emphasize the transformative power of sympathy as compromise: what is a curtailment of civil liberty and rights becomes a one-off social dispute at best, a family matter at worst. This is an integral part of government by contradistinction, a mode of security rule. This logic severs connection and inhibits the formation of solidarities, even as it creates its own interconnected geography of national security. The protest's attempt to name and critique the slippery, slow violence of India's security regime at this friendly border is turned into a pedagogical moment. *Because* it is a friendly border, sympathy can be expected, indeed, even made obligatory since borderland citizens and BSF soldiers recognize each other's struggles and sacrifices. *Because* of this friendliness, the anger of alienation and radical politics of humiliation is out of place and cannot be heard, not least because of the longer temporality of injustice and violence it archives. This is simply no place for protest.

Domesticating National Security

Membership in the heteropatriarchal Indian family-nation necessarily involves a degree of sacrifice, unequally demanded of its different constituents. The "family trope," writes Anne McClintock, is crucial for nationalism because it offers a "natural" metaphor "sanctioning national *hierarchy* within a putative organic *unity* of interests."[42] As Muslims and as borderland residents, this call for sympathy and compromise reaffirms their suffering and the subservience of democratic rights under the sign of security state as "normal" and to be endured, even expected. This is not the suffering of soldiers that merits recognition as heroes and martyrs; this is the suffering of subordinated members such as women in the family, the sacrifices they must offer in lieu of their being deemed deserving of the gift of citizenship in a security state where they are always already suspect. While McClintock offers a close reading of Frantz Fanon to highlight the "naturalness of nationalism as a domestic genealogy,"[43] this instance is an example of how this genealogy extends to constituting the normality and the fundamentally patriarchal authority of national security. The Muslim citizen cast as "the wife at home" must mother and suffer the errant male in order to remain in the family; the burden of keeping peace in the heteropatriarchal family-nation is on this feminized citizen-subject. Heteropatriarchal family relations of power not only furnish the language of friendliness but naturalize and domesticate the cunning of liberal engagement through which the Indian security regime maintains the fiction of democratic inclusion.

The domestication of national security travels through another genealogy yet. Writing about revolutionary acts in Egypt, anthropologist Jessica Winegar questions the gendered and classed assumptions that underlie the iconic figure and space of revolution, noting that "everyday domestic experiences are crucial for the public staging of claims."[44] This intervention is a critical reminder of the continuous investment—in this case by the security state—in the public/private binary to police what is *properly* political. The invocation of scalar equivalences of the family-nation as apposite to a friendly national security location configures a public act, an instance of state violence, as a personal one. The soldier's anger expressed while on active duty and in uniform is rationalized through his personal familial circumstances and reactions of anger also recast in the same language. The outline of the nation as family circumscribes the sol-diering son as a family member to be disciplined through informal disciplinary measures. The emotions of anger and humiliation that it stirs in the community and which find expression through collective action are radically threatening in its "dissensus": for it stakes claim to "a possible world in which the argument could count as an argument, one that is addressed by a subject qualified to argue, over an identified object, to an addressee who is required to see the object and to hear the argument that he 'normally' has no reason either to see or to hear."[45]

Dissenting locals used the terms *protest (protibaad)*, *movement (andolan)*, *injustice (anyay)*, and *judgment (bichar)* to characterize the incident, their response to it and expectations from the collective action. However, BSF and local political leaders referred to it as "troubles" (*jhamela* or *harkat*), a "misunderstanding" (*bhul bojha-bujhi*), "anger" that had been resolved with "explanation" (Hindi *samjhana*, Bengali *bojha-pora*). The denial of political agency by refusing to recognize actions as protests or to "dele-gitimize even criminalize those who act outside limited repertoires of non-violent" actions is a hallmark of state repression.[46] Unequal speaking positions testify, as Papori Bora writes in her analysis of the crisis of talks between India and its insurgent Northeast, to "a continued history of failed conversations." She notes that the liberal political technique of "dialogue" itself is a tactic of concealment that more ostensibly demo-cratic engagements cannot resolve.[47] The protesters' demand for a formal inquiry in which their elected political representatives and members of the civil administration also participate is dismissed as too serious and inappropriate for what is "an intimate matter" (*aapas ka mamla*). The injury then is located within civil-military relations that are recast as inti-mate, kin-like, to be resolved also within that sphere. The Muslim citizen is placed in the precarious position of being responsible for wanting to disturb that intimacy, its balance always fragile and tentative. Here the invocation of the nation as family, with subordination being the price of inclusion for some members, dramatizes the tensions at the core of India's secular liberal democracy.

The position—in geopolitical, affective, and discursive senses—of the "friendly border" is thus produced in a relation of contradistinction to places of insurgency, conflict, and hostility in India's national security geography. As scholars of publics and counterpublics note, every protest creates a "we," necessarily enacting insider/outsider boundaries.[48] The "we" of this blockade is not the same "we" of BSF's national security/family. That slippage is instructive about the affective economy of friendliness: how it attempts to fuse collectives with collectives, obfuscating the dissonances. For the BSF, their effective and affective presence in these eastern borderlands is constructed interreferentially through contrasts and comparisons with other locations in India's national security geography. Friendliness demands an emotional connection of sympathy and prefigures acceptable forms of political expression—namely, the dialogue. The politics of contradistinction work to contain residents of the friendly border in an ascribed position in the Indian national family as well as a speaking position within a dialogue. Through its dialogic intervention, border citizens are constituted as empathetically capable, to be reasoned with, to be tutored into the hierarchies of the national security-family. Absolved of radical alterity, their inclusion within the national fold is strictly conditional on maintaining their positions with the affective economy of friendliness.

Let us return to the question of difference in protests against security regimes. How can we widen the notion of protest to consider that which entails (unresolved) epistemic inquiries about security regimes and their religious and gendered logics? Winegar notes that to question who can be revolutionary and how is not simply to look for agency of women's work but to rethink the privileges of normative revolutionary acts.[49] Likewise, to question what a protest is and who can be a legitimate protester is not to search for acts of resistance in the template of dominant modes and forms of political action. The gathered crowd of men and women angrily protesting thus threaten that figure of the suffering and feminized religious minority citizen and its very terms of inclusion as appeasing the Hindu majoritarian security state. Their protest, foregrounding *cumulative* humiliation, not simply a single instance, sketches out the religious and gendered logics of the security state's violence. Read this way, the articulation of collective humiliation is astute political critique.

For days after the blockade at the checkpoint, borderland residents remained confused and uncertain about its status. The "standpoints of the subjugated are not 'innocent' positions," Donna Haraway reminds us.[50] Indeed, residents disagreed and wrestled with ambivalences among themselves as much as they did with the BSF, though that is another story. Borderland residents, then, in insisting on describing their action as protest and their mobilization as a movement, were calling the bluff of the security state's template of "dialogue" and cooperation. The expression of humiliation itself becomes a contestation as a new "public space of appearance . . . a new 'between' of bodies" is made possible;[51] the circulation of friendliness as a structuring affect, commanding sympathy and repressing outrage, is obstructed. Inhabiting and owning the humiliation and injury suffered by Hasan Ali, collectively enabled Muslim borderland residents a space and time to mobilize what they experience as sedimented negative emotions into something powerful that the security state was forced to attend to. The BSF officer's attempt to introduce lighthearted humor into the "dialogue" by using the analogy of wife and workplace is not merely a joke in poor taste. Both humiliation and sympathy here show powerfully that "emotions *do things*, and they align individuals with communities—or bodily space with social space."[52] An explicit refusal of the metaphorically—and unapologetically violent—intimate domain to characterize the kind of civil-military interactions that unfold, the young man's agitation pushed back on being cast as the emasculated victim. Challenging the epistemic, affective, and political horizons defined by friendliness, to name the blockade a "movement" or "protest" was to recognize its subjects as political actors. It made a mess of a plot for the security state. Staying with the troubled and troubling small voice of protest can perhaps surface a connected geography of outrage beyond its locality while also paying close attention to how humiliation brought everyone together that morning at the checkpoint.

Sahana Ghosh is assistant professor of anthropology at the National University of Singapore. Her work on militarization, gender, borderlands, and the politics of mobility within South Asia has been published in *American Anthropologist*, *Comparative Studies of South Asia, Africa, and the Middle East*, and *Gender, Place, and Culture*, among other journals. Her work has also been published in public outlets such as *Border Criminologies*, *The Conversation*, and *Café Dissensus*.

Notes

This essay has grown and changed over many years: it owes much to the questions and feedback from participants at the workshop Religion, Gender, and the Politics of Security at Yale University in 2019, the Feminist Preconference at the Annual Conference on South Asia at the University of Wisconsin–Madison in 2017, and the Political Anthropology Working Group at Harvard University. Thanks especially to Lila Abu-Lughod, Samar al-Bulushi, Anjali Arondekar, Inderpal Grewal, Deepti

Misri, Tanmoy Sharma, and Ajantha Subramanian for vital queries on different versions. To my friends in Cooch Behar: maybe it left a mark? Thank you for everything.

1. My long-term fieldwork is in Cooch Behar district, West Bengal, and I also draw on research experience in other rural borderlands of West Bengal. The experience and nature of militarization along the 4,096-kilometer-long border is regionally varied, a point integral to my larger argument about a differentiated national security geography. For militarization in the northeastern parts of the same border where distinct political ecologies and dynamics of race, religion, and gender play out, see Kikon, *Living with Oil and Coal*; McDuie-Ra, "Fifty-Year Disturbance."

2. The Border Security Force is a paramilitary organization raised in 1965 for the purpose of securing India's international borders. Trained militarily to be battle ready, it is currently in charge of guarding India's borders with Pakistan and Bangladesh and deployed in counterinsurgency operations from Kashmir to central India.

3. See van Schendel, *Bengal Borderlands*.

4. See Sur, "In the Name."

5. See S. Ghosh, "'Everything Must Match.'"

6. The Bengali words used were *opoman* and *beijjat*, which could be read as humiliation and disrespect, respectively.

7. English words in italics were used as such in Bengali—or, in this case, Hindi—speech.

8. For a critical analysis of the dominance of visuality in South Asian political forms, see Mitchell, "Visual Turn."

9. See for instance, Tawil-Souri, "It's Still about the Power"; Abu-Lughod, "Living the 'Revolution'"; Zaidi and Pani, "If on a Winter's Night."

10. This incident was reported only in two Bengali newspapers and one news channel local to northern West Bengal. I only knew about it because I was living in these border villages at that time and was summoned to the blockade to photograph it and serve as a translator/interpreter between Hindi and Bengali during the dialogue. Had I been on the adjacent Bangladeshi side—which I periodically was through this same period—I might have missed this incident altogether.

11. Ranajit Guha's celebrated essay "A Small Voice of History" is foundational to the work of the Subaltern Studies Group that sought to read colonial archives otherwise in order to craft peasant histories.

12. See Cohen, Forbis, and Misri, "Protest."

13. See Bhaumik, *Troubled Periphery*. Kashmir is frequently referred to as a burning or troubled "paradise" in journalistic accounts, while the India-Bangladesh border is described as "porous" in both English-language media and parliamentary debates in India.

14. Students inside the Jamia Milia Islamia University Library were teargassed by the Delhi Police in December 2019 for protesting amendments to the secular basis of citizenship in India. Indian security forces shot to blind and maim Kashmiris in a new lethal tactic of violence through the summer of 2016; see Misri, "Dark Ages and Bright Futures." For an extended discussion of the sixteen-year-long fast by Iron Sharmila, "unseen" by the political center in India, see Bora, "Speech of the Nation."

15. See Ali et al., "Geographies of Occupation."

16. See Alexander, Chatterjee, and Jalais, *Bengal Diaspora*; Roy, *Partitioned Lives*.

17. See Datta, *Refugees and Borders*.

18. See A. Ghosh, "India's 9/11?"

19. Amnesty India's website Halt the Hate tracks alleged hate crimes and in 2018, for example, found over two hundred cases against Dalits and Muslims (*Hindu*, "Amnesty Report").

20. See Chatterjee, "Religious Minorities"; Sarkar, *Hindu Wife, Hindu Nation*.

21. For seminal collections on this topic, see Abu-Lughod and Lutz, *Language and the Politics of Emotions*; Yuval-Davis and Anthias, *Women-Nation-State*; Kaplan, Alarcon, and Moallem, *Between Woman and Nation*.

22. Sundar, "'Winning Hearts and Minds,'" 708.

23. Sundar, "'Winning Hearts and Minds.'"

24. See Khalili, "Uses of Happiness." I follow Ann Pellegrini and Jasbir Puar, who note in "Affect" that what runs through recent critical approaches to affect—despite their use of different terms such as *emotions, feelings, sensations*—is to probe its relation toward political acts and ends. Like them, I am less interested in delimiting terms and instead welcome the generative flow that these analytical genealogies allow.

25. See Ahmed, "Affective Economies."

26. While illegal immigration from Bangladesh to India across this border has been a long-standing and bipartisan political issue, successive right-wing Hindu governments have mobilized the figure of the illegal migrant as synonymous with Bangladeshi Muslim. See Gillan, "Refugees or Infiltrators?"; S. Ghosh, "Everything Must Match."

27. Thomas Blom Hansen, in "The Political Theology of Violence," emphasizes the trope of fire and spontaneous combustion in mobilizing crowds. For an overview of outrage in social movements in India, see also Blom and Jaoul, "Introduction."

28. See Butler, *Notes Toward a Performative Theory*.

29. I have made this argument extensively in S. Ghosh, "Security Socialities."

30. See Chen, "Agitation," 551.

31. See Sachar Committee, "Social, Economic, and Educational Status."

32. Maidul Islam, in "Rethinking the Muslim Question," argues that questions of socioeconomic class and inequality are fundamental to the community identity of Muslims in India.

33. See Guru, "Introduction," 5.

34. See Palshikar, "Understanding Humiliation."

35. See Guru, "Introduction," 18.

36. See Abu-Lughod, "Living the 'Revolution.'"

37. See S. Ghosh, "Security Socialities."

38. See Chen, "Agitation," 563.

39. See Bora, "Between the Human"; Sundar, "Winning Hearts and Minds"; Misri, "'Are You a Man?'"

40. See Zia, "Killable Kashmiri Body."

41. See Baxi, *Public Secrets*, 183.

42. See McClintock, "'No Longer in a Future Heaven,'" 93.

43. McClintock, "'No Longer in a Future Heaven,'" 93. She notes how remarkable Fanon was in recognizing early on that "militarization and the centralization of authority in a country automatically entail a resurgence of the authority of the father" (Fanon, *Black Skin, White Masks*, 141–42).

44. Winegar, "Privilege of Revolution," 68.

45. Rancière, "Ten Theses," 39.

46. Cohen, Forbis, and Misri, "Protest," 17.

47. See Bora, "Speech of the Nation," 672.

48. See Warner, "Publics and Counterpublics"; Chowdhury, *Paradoxes of the Popular*; Cody, "Publics and Politics."

49. Winegar, "Privilege of Revolution."

50. See Haraway, "Situated Knowledges," 584.

51. Butler, *Towards a Performative Theory.*

52. See Ahmed, "Affective Economies," 119.

References

Abu-Lughod, Lila. "Living the 'Revolution' in an Egyptian Village: Moral Action in a National Space." *American Ethnologist* 39, no. 1 (2012): 21–25.

Abu-Lughod, Lila, and Catherine Lutz, eds. *Language and the Politics of Emotions.* Cambridge: Cambridge University Press, 2008.

Ahmed, Sara. "Affective Economies." *Social Text*, no. 79 (2004): 117–39.

Alexander, Claire, Joya Chatterji, and Annu Jalais. *The Bengal Diaspora: Muslim Migrants in Britain, India, and Bangladesh.* London: Routledge. 2014.

Ali, Nosheen, et al. "Geographies of Occupation in South Asia." *Feminist Studies* 45, nos. 2–3 (2019): 574–80.

Baxi, Pratiksha. *Public Secrets of Law: Rape Trials in India.* New Delhi: Oxford University Press, 2014.

Bhaumik, Subir. *Troubled Periphery: Crisis of India's North East.* New Delhi: Sage, 2009.

Blom, Amelie, and Nicolas Jaoul. "Introduction: The Moral and Affectual Dimension of Collective Action in South Asia." *South Asia Multidisciplinary Academic Journal* 2 (2008): 1–25.

Bora, Papori. "Between the Human, the Citizen, and the Tribal." *International Journal of Feminist Politics* 12, nos. 3–4 (2010): 341–60.

Bora, Papori. "Speech of the Nation and Conversations at the Margins of the Nation-State." *Interventions* 17, no. 5 (2015): 669–85.

Butler, Judith. *Notes Toward a Performative Theory of Assembly.* Cambridge, MA: Harvard University Press, 2015.

Chen, Mel Y. "Agitation." *South Atlantic Quarterly* 117, no. 3 (2018): 551–66.

Chatterjee, Partha. "Religious Minorities and the Secular State: Reflections on an Indian Impasse." *Public Culture* 8, no. 1 (1995): 11–39.

Chowdhury, Nusrat Sabina. *Paradoxes of the Popular: Crowd Politics in Bangladesh.* Stanford, CA: Stanford University Press, 2019.

Cody, Francis. "Publics and Politics." *Annual Review of Anthropology* 40, no. 1 (2011): 37–52.

Cohen, Elena, Melissa Forbis, and Deepti Misri. "Introduction: Protest." *WSQ* 46, nos. 3–4 (2018): 14–27.

Datta, Antara. *Refugees and Borders in South Asia: The Great Exodus of 1971.* London: Routledge, 2012.

Fanon, Frantz. *Black Skin, White Masks.* London: Pluto, 1986.

Ghosh, Amitav. "India's 9/11? Not Exactly." *New York Times*, December 3, 2008.

Ghosh, Sahana. "'Everything Must Match': Detection, Deception, and Migrant Illegality in the India-Bangladesh Borderlands." *American Anthropologist* 121, no. 4 (2019): 870–83.

Ghosh, Sahana. "Security Socialities: Gender, Surveillance, and Civil-Military Relations in India's Eastern Borderlands." *Comparative Studies of South Asia, Africa and the Middle East* 39, no. 3 (2019): 439–50.

Gillan, Michael. "Refugees or Infiltrators? The Bharatiya Janata Party and 'Illegal' Migration from Bangladesh." *Asian Studies Review* 26, no. 1 (2002): 73–95.

Guha, Ranajit. "A Small Voice of History." In *The Small Voice of History: Collected Essays*, 304–17. Ranikhet: Permanent Black, 2010.

Guru, Gopal, "Introduction: Theorizing Humiliation." In *Humiliation: Claims and Contexts*, edited by Gopal Guru, 1–19. New Delhi: Oxford University Press, 2009.

Hansen, Thomas Blom. "The Political Theology of Violence in Contemporary India." *South Asia Multidisciplinary Academic Journal*, no. 2 (2008). https://doi.org/10.4000/samaj.1872.

Haraway, Donna. "Situated Knowledges." *Feminist Studies* 14, no. 3 (1988): 575–99.

Hindu. "Amnesty Report." October 4, 2019. https://www.thehindu.com/news/national/amnesty-report-hate-crimes-rose-sharply-the-first-half-of-2019/article29598191.ece.

Islam, Maidul. "Rethinking the Muslim Question in Post-colonial India." *Social Scientist* 40, nos. 7–8 (2012): 61–84.

Kaplan, Caren, Norma Alarcon, and Minoo Moallem, eds. *Between Woman and Nation: Nationalisms, Transnationalism Feminisms, and the State.* Durham, NC: Duke University Press, 1999.

Khalili, Laleh. "The Uses of Happiness in Counterinsurgencies." *Social Text*, no. 118 (2014): 23–43.

Kikon, Dolly. *Living with Oil and Coal: Resource Politics and Militarization in Northeast India.* Seattle: University of Washington Press, 2019.

McClintock, Anne. "'No Longer in a Future Heaven': Gender, Race, and Nationalism." In *Dangerous Liaisons: Gender, Nation, and Postcolonial Perspectives*, edited by Anne McClintock, Aamir Mufti, and Ella Shohat, 89–112. Minneapolis: University of Minnesota Press, 1997.

McDuie-Ra, Duncan. "Fifty-Year Disturbance: The Armed Forces Special Powers Act and Exceptionalism in a South Asian Periphery." *Contemporary South Asia* 17, no. 3 (2009): 255–70.

Misri, Deepti. "'Are You a Man?': Performing Naked Protest in India." *Signs* 36, no. 3 (2011): 603–25.

Misri, Deepti. "Dark Ages and Bright Futures: Youth, Disability, and Time in Kashmir." *Public Culture*, no. 92 (2020): 539–65.

Mitchell, Lisa. "The Visual Turn in Political Anthropology and the Mediation of Political Practice in Contemporary India." *South Asia* 37, no. 3 (2014): 515–40.

Palshikar, Sanjay. "Understanding Humiliation." In *Humiliation: Claims and Contexts*, edited by Gopal Guru, 79–92. New Delhi: Oxford University Press, 2009.

Pellegrini, Ann, and Jasbir Puar. "Affect." *Social Text*, no. 100 (2009): 35–38.

Rancière, Jacques. "Ten Theses on Politics." In *Dissensus: On Politics and Aesthetics*, edited and translated by Steven Corcoran, 35–52. London: Bloomsbury, 2010.

Roy, Haimanti. *Partitioned Lives: Migrants, Refugees, and Citizens in India and Pakistan, 1947–65.* New York: Oxford University Press. 2013.

Sachar Committee. "Social, Economic, and Educational Status of the Muslim Community in India." Government of India. 2006.

Sarkar, Tanika. *Hindu Wife, Hindu Nation: Community, Religion, and Cultural Nationalism.* Bloomington: Indiana University Press, 2001.

Sundar, Nandini. "'Winning Hearts and Minds': Emotional Wars and the Construction of Difference." *Third World Quarterly* 33, no. 4 (2012): 705–20.

Sur, Malini. "In the Name of Indian Citizenship? Criminalizing Statelessness at the India-Bangladesh Border." *Border Criminologies* (blog), February 17, 2020. Centre for Criminology, University of Oxford. https://www.law.ox.ac.uk/research-subject-groups/centre-criminology/centreborder-criminologies/blog/2020/02/name-indian.

Tawil-Suri, Helga. "It's Still about the Power of Place." *Middle East Journal of Culture and Communication* 5, no. 1 (2012): 86–95.

Van Schendel, Willem. *The Bengal Borderlands: Beyond State and Nation in South Asia.* London: Anthem Press. 2005.

Warner, Michael. "Publics and Counterpublics." *Public Culture* 14, no. 1 (2002): 49–90.

Winegar, Jessica. "The Privilege of Revolution: Gender, Class, Space, and Affect in Egypt." *American Ethnologist* 39, no. 1 (2012): 67–70.

Yuval-Davis, Nira, and Floya Anthias, eds. *Women-Nation-State.* London: Macmillan, 1989.

Zaidi, Sarover, and Samprati Pani. "If on a Winter's Night, Azadi . . ." *Chiragh Dilli* (blog), February 15, 2020. https://chiraghdilli.com/2020/02/15/if-on-a-winters-night-azadi/.

Zia, Ather. "The Killable Kashmiri Body: The Life and Execution of Afzal Guru." In *Resisting Occupation in Kashmir,* edited by Haley Duschinski, Mona Bhan, Ather Zin, and Cynthia Mahmood, 103–28. Philadelphia: University of Pennsylvania Press, 2018.

The Security State and Securitizing Patriarchies in Postcolonial India

Inderpal Grewal, Dipin Kaur, Sasha Sabherwal

The period of the 1980s and 1990s was a time of insurgency and state counterinsurgency in Indian Punjab, though it was by no means the only challenge to the Indian state since its independence in 1947. Conflicts inside the country as well as on the borders emerged in the Northeast and Kashmir as well as in regions such as Chhattisgarh, where Maoist movements erupted to fight the Indian state. The borders of the postcolonial state, as well as some of its interior regions, continue to challenge the state as a stable entity.[1] Similar to other regions of Africa and the Middle East that have been created by colonial boundary making and partitioning, the project of national security in India has led to border conflicts, animosities, and anxieties that have come to characterize the postcolonial state. These anxieties have meant that state repression—policing, militarizing, and securitizing—continue to be used to hold together people as a nation whose territorial boundary was imposed from the outside and by outsiders. Punjab is one example in India whose geography reveals the violence of the postcolonial state as it struggled to produce a nation through its repression of insurgencies that unsettled the partitioned subcontinent.

The case of Punjab suggests that the specificity of securitization in Asia, Africa, the Middle East, and the Caribbean emerges from a colonial history, and a colonial legacy of policing and law and order deployed for state repression in the ongoing project to make a nation-state out of colonial partitioning. Adding to that historical legacy of imperialism, the pressures of ongoing and contemporary geopolitics also inform security regimes in neoimperial ways, especially through the US-produced "global war on terror." In such security projects, constructions of gender that emerge from colonialism are in constant deployment, recruiting commu-

DOI 10.1215/01642472-9771077

nities and families into the colonial and postcolonial state through both biopolitical and necropolitical futures.

Even as other border uprisings continue in Kashmir and India's Northeast, the conflict in Punjab is, by all accounts, perceived as a "success" for the Indian state against the Sikh insurgency. Over the following decades, the "Punjab Solution" has provided a blueprint for counterinsurgency operations elsewhere.[2] Despite this claim of success, scholarly debates about the impacts of the insurgency and the counterinsurgency continue into the present.[3] The insurgent movement that erupted in Punjab, similarly, continues as aspirational for some groups (even outside the region), but also serves as reason for continued security presence in the region due to concerns by the Indian state that "militancy" or "terrorism" may rise up again. Moreover, the global war on terror, a project of the United States as it emerged over the last two decades, reanimates concern over "terrorists," as Sikh insurgents came to be labeled by the state. The constant threat of labeling dissident groups as terrorists has become the defining aspect of contemporary security states. In the process, South Asian regional politics, especially the relations with Pakistan and Afghanistan, have been entangled in the geopolitics of this global war, leading to continued military clashes and territorial disputes with Pakistan, and more recently, China.

The emergence of Sikh nationalism (often termed "ethno-nationalism") led by Jarnail Singh Bhindranwale in the late 1970s was built on economic and religious grievances that began in the colonial period and continued after independence. Negotiations among British and Indian nationalist leaders in the 1940s led to the division of Punjab between India and Pakistan, setting the stage for the traumatic and bloody event of Partition that inaugurated the new nation. Decades later, the insurgency of Punjab in the 1980s was suppressed by the central government through the use of militarized forces, the creation of antiterrorist laws such as the Terrorist and Disruptive Activities (Prevention) Act (TADA) of 1987, and the deployment of brutal police violence against the Sikh community. Some estimate that twenty-five thousand people were killed, many at the hands of security forces.[4] Nearly three decades later, while Kashmir, the Northeast, and the Maoist "Red Corridor" are seen as spaces of state violence and unrest, Punjab is believed to be at peace because of a successful counterinsurgency. Yet these narratives of "peace" or "success" do not account for the ongoing gendered, political, and economic violence in Punjab.[5] Sikh nationalist aspirations remain ongoing among some groups (and especially in diasporic spaces), while the state's economy, mainly rural, remains in shambles, and its youth are leaving the region.[6] The lack of jobs and employment has led to migrations abroad and to shifting geographies of urban and rural life in Punjab.[7]

This article examines postcolonial violence through a gendered approach—that is, through understanding impacts on and shifts in patriarchies and masculinities that have continuities across the colonial and postcolonial state. We draw on semistructured interviews from fieldwork in Punjab across three summers between 2016 and 2018, textual analysis of primary sources, human rights reports, and news articles to explore religious reform and the paternalistic masculinities of key political actors: Jarnail Singh Bhindranwale (the leader of the insurgency), K. P. S. Gill (the police chief), and Beant Singh (chief minister from 1992 to 1995). While there is now a great deal of scholarship on the period of the 1980s in Punjab, especially on emerging Sikh nationalisms,[8] few studies have examined the effects of gendered violence from this period of insurgency. Research by Rainuka Dagar does address this gap, but it focuses predominantly on the experiences of women, whereas our focus is to examine the structures of patriarchy and masculinity that are also central to research on gender.[9] Specifically, we argue that the regimes of precolonial and colonial militarism, which constructed hegemonic notions of Sikh masculinity in service to the colonial and postcolonial state, were altered in this period, and a dominant caste-based warrior masculinity came to be fractured to include a more securitized version. Our research reveals that hegemonic Sikh masculinities were altered but remained powerful during this time as the patriarchal state and patriarchal communities both relied on violence for their own ends. We see the targeting of Sikhs, a religious minority and a border community, as part of the broader process of postcolonial nation making through militarism and security that alters the nature of its patriarchy, and we reveal that such masculinities are central to emerging practices of security across state and society.[10] While this article focuses on masculinities and patriarchies, we note that the overwhelming contest between state and insurgent patriarchies leaves many others—especially women and those of other genders and castes—in the region to suffer the violence, one that people do not easily forget.[11]

Over the span of a decade in Punjab, the Indian Army, paramilitary forces, and state police carried out a combination of "cordon and search" operations, arrests, and abductions with impunity using special counterinsurgency laws which targeted any identifiable male Sikhs. Jats, one of the most powerful castes in Punjab due to their ownership of land and property and control of Sikh religious institutions, were particularly targeted, especially those in rural areas. The accused were implicated in false cases, subjected to torture, sexual harassment, and assault, or forcefully disappeared, extrajudicially executed, and illegally cremated with impunity.[12] Furthermore, the insurgency itself recuperated a history of patriarchal nationalism, religious reform, and mostly male figures of religious authority in order to gain power in the region. The confluence of multiple sedimented and emergent masculinities and patriarchies (of the postcolonial Indian state and within the region) produced forms of gender and power that fueled the insurgency as well as the counterinsurgency, leading to economic, political, and social changes in the region that continue to resonate into the present.

Patriarchy and the Colonial and Postcolonial State

Feminist scholars such as Urvashi Butalia and Veena Das have underscored the founding moment of independence as based on patriarchal logics that undergirded some of the violence of Partition.[13] If we understand patriarchy as a form of structural violence built into the Indian state from its founding moments, we need to also examine how it shifts and changes over time,[14] and interrogate the intimacy between state and community patriarchies. Because state structures are also cultural formations, they are difficult to hold accountable precisely because they are embedded within particular cultures and are not alien to them.

Punjab has been seen as a region characterized by patriarchy, one that is based on caste and property. Punjabi patriarchy and masculinity have long been hypervisible as a stereotype and historical formation produced through religion, class, and caste. What one might call a masculinist overdetermination is central to these narratives of Sikh identity and communalism. For many scholars and politicians in both India and outside, the male turban-wearing Sikh represents the community,[15] an image that has limitations because of the plural history of the region.[16] Within India, that figure is the target of jokes as much as it is seen as a threat in the West. The emergence of Jats as the dominant caste group further emphasizes a particular version of masculinity that endures to this day in popular culture in the region and elsewhere.[17]

Punjab's precolonial history as a region of war, religious transformation, and struggle, and the powerful Sikh kingdom of Ranjit Singh as able to withstand British power, all combined to produce a martial tradition that became useful to British control of the subcontinent.[18] The colonial state built on this history, constructing Sikh men (of the Jat caste and from rural areas in particular) as good soldiers and warriors who were inducted in large numbers into the British army, producing a notion of the "martial caste" and "martial races."[19] Through this process, Sikhs, mostly of the Jat caste, were recast in masculine archetype as hardy, warlike, enduring, and loyal. In an attempt to continue recruiting from the community, the colonial state permitted the possession of religious swords (*kirpans*) among Sikhs (figured as men) in the military, and relied on their turbans and beards as signs of warrior masculinity. At the same time, as Sikhs became visible in both the colonial state and in anticolonial resistance, the same markers of martial status also became symbols of anticolonial resistance.[20] Sikh men remained visible as soldiers in the first few decades after independence, becoming nationally visible as embodiments of Otherness, protection, and threat.[21] Within the Sikh community, Jats constituted the dominant caste patriarchy in the region, their visibility and power—in politics and as the majority of rural landowners in a predominantly agricultural state—often erasing the presence of Punjabi women, and its religious and caste heterogeneity.

During the period of insurgency, these militarized masculinities were transformed and split in close relation to the masculinity of the state. First, Sikh males were transformed from the warrior protecting the nation and community into the figure of the terrorist and the extremist. According to Steven Wilkinson, three districts in Punjab's Majha region where much of the insurgent violence was concentrated during the conflict—Amritsar, Tarn Taran, and Gurdaspur—were also the three most heavily recruited army districts in India, with more than one hundred thousand army veterans and thousands more serving army *jawans* (junior soldiers) and officers even today.[22] Such a history reveals the overlap between the state-sponsored militarized masculinity and the masculinity of the insurgency.

Second, this same masculinity became securitized as Sikh men in the police force were asked by the state to carry out a counterinsurgency against others in their religious and caste community.[23] Since the very beginning of the counterinsurgency campaign, Sikh males have been at its helm as much as they have also been leaders in the insurgency. The Indian Army's June 1984 attack (code-named Operation Bluestar by the state) on Sikhism's most revered place of worship[24] and its subsequent targeting of rural Sikh youth in their homes in the countryside (code-named Operation Woodrose), created a rupture between the Sikhs and the Indian Army's disproportionate use of force, which further fueled insurgent sympathies among the local population.[25] Two of the generals leading Operation Bluestar[26] and the president of India, Zail Singh, as well as their prime target, the leader of the insurgency, Jarnail Singh Bhindranwale, were Sikh males, mostly from the Jat caste,[27] as was the police chief, K. P. S. Gill. Army units with high Sikh representation were used for visible public works projects along the volatile border belt, and Punjab police commandos were encouraged to keep visible symbols of Sikhism (such as a beard and a neatly tied headdress).[28] In an attempt to improve the resonance and acceptance of the Army and police within Punjab's rural Sikh community, a securitized construction of Sikh masculinity was enabled by the state in order to control the region.[29]

A third version of masculinity is of the paternal and protective patriarchs, who became victims of the state, as did a religious and reformist masculinity. The former masculinity was transformed into the patriarchal keeper of religious tradition, while the latter became the subject of a new piety and the enemy of the state. Religiously observant or locally powerful masculinities became seen as terrorists and enemies of the state. Such differences were not just in the realm of theology or ideology, but also visible in sartorial performance: the military and police style of tying up beards neatly and turbans in somber shades, and wearing uniforms comprising pants and shirts, was quite distinct from the insurgency's bright yellow turbans and flowing kurtas. Such differences were most visible between the two powerful male figures around whom this masculinist conflict revolved, where Jarnail Singh Bhindranwale emerged as the insurgent reformer, while K. P. S. Gill was celebrated for "stamping out terrorism."[30]

Religious Reform and Paternal Masculinities: Jarnail Singh Bhindranwale

Jarnail Singh Bhindranwale, head of the orthodox Sikh religious school Damdami Taksal, became the key figure in the Khalistan (Sikh separatist) movement. His masculinity was performed in religious terms through the charismatic authority of "*babas*," the holy man or the spiritual leader of a religious sect who sits in his particular site within the "*deras*" (sectarian religious communities).[31] Bhindranwale combined his nationalism with a longer tradition of the "*baba*" and the moral reform of religion that first emerged in early twentieth-century India within Hindu, Muslim, and Sikh reform movements.[32] His image was of a tall man, youthfully dressed in white robe with a blue turban and flowing beard, and his speeches circulated powerfully, especially in the form of cassette tapes that could be found across Punjab and its diasporas.[33] He spoke in a language that refracted religious history through contemporary politics (and economic issues) to produce a nationalism that resonated with many in the rural areas who were tired of the corruption of politicians and government policies and were concerned with what they saw as the central government's discriminatory treatment of agricultural issues in Punjab. His speeches referenced Sikhs as a rural, unified, and masculine community, but one that needed reform and purification to become "true" Sikhs. Both these formations—the religious reformer and the spiritual leader—reproduced masculinities emerging from both Sikh history and the colonial and postcolonial state that entrenched male power within an ongoing politics of state power and negotiations with the central government.

While his following did not extend to all Sikhs or across all castes of Sikhs, the state counterinsurgency and government actions (particularly the Indian military attack on Sikhs' holiest religious site, the Golden Temple) created sympathy for Bhindranwale in rural areas of Punjab and in diasporic spaces that emerged variously in Europe and North America.[34] To this day, his memory remains alive among certain segments of the Sikh community in Punjab and its diasporas, visible in photographs, T-shirts, calendars, and other such popular items in the "bazaar economy," and as commodities and icons.[35] His iconicity extends to making ethnic identity in North America and political campaigns in Punjab, as well as social and national aspirations for diasporic and Punjab-based groups across the world. In Punjab he is remembered by both Hindus and Sikhs—especially rural, small-town, and middle-class women—more for his respectability and reformist politics than for his nationalist aspirations.[36] Bhindranwale, like his fellow *"sants"* (saints), could not expand his following across all castes and communities, even among Sikhs.[37] The plural history of Punjab[38] could not easily be attached to his version of Sikh nationalism, even as his image and memory proliferates as it is used by political parties to gain votes.

We saw this understanding of Bhindranwale in our ethnographic research.[39] In another article, we address the language that women use to describe Bhindranwale and his followers' approaches to the conflict.[40] What is important to note is that while the media and popular culture used terms like *atankvadi* or *Attwadi* (one who creates terror) to refer to Bhindranwale, our informants used terms such as *kharku* (one who creates disturbance), but they did not always use them pejoratively. Women also used the term *baba* (holy man, or spiritual leader) because Bhindranwale was seen to be a holy man with religious authority. Thus, our interlocutors referred to these men as *babas*, while the state termed them terrorists or criminals. Women saw Sikh men as targets of the state even as they remembered and valued the history of reform that Bhindranwale brought—a memory that is shared among many Sikh, Hindu, and Dalit religious communities. Many mourned the loss of sons, fathers, and male relatives killed or imprisoned, or those who had migrated. However, they also recalled, with approval, the kinds of moral reform and politics of purity that the insurgency promised: simple marriages without dowry, attire that did not require the consumption that marked the present, abstention from alcohol and drugs, devotion to prayer, and purification of religious practice.

These moral structures have long been used by various religious leaders in religious reform movements since the twentieth century, and *"babas"* and *"deras"* use these ideals to enlist and discipline followers. Gender respectability was remembered with nostalgia by our informants who recalled when women wore modest dress and exhibited modest behavior.[41] Importantly, even as many had remembered that Bhindranwale's movement had helped women by regulating male consumption of alcohol and drugs, they also remembered that women were disciplined, often in violent ways, rendering them vulnerable to sexual assault by insurgents and other groups who took on the mantle of Bhindranwale, as well as by the police.[42] These religious reforms, whether understood by our interlocutors as nostalgic or as disciplining, were constitutive of Bhindranwale's paternalism, which brought together religious reform with a nationalist and revolutionary masculinity.

Shifting Masculinities: K. P. S. Gill and the Production of Security Expertise

There is irony in the fact that, as political scientist Jugdep Chima points out, the same honorific of *baba* used for the insurgent leader, Bhindranwale, was also used by subordinates to refer to both police chief, K. P. S. Gill, and the chief minister of Punjab at the time, Beant Singh.[43] This was a deliberate effort by the state to reappropriate insurgent symbols, local identities, loyalties, and respect. Gill worked to co-opt both Sikh and Bhindranwale's cultural symbols and motifs across the security apparatus, presenting himself as a better representative of the Sikh community. This kind of mirroring of patriarchy and power produced contestations between insurgency and counterinsurgency, and between a patriarchal reformist movement for Sikh nationalism and the patriarchal state. Yet both relied on violence and masculinity to control the population.

K. P. S. Gill, who came to call himself a "security expert," is celebrated even decades later across India for "stamping out terrorism."[44] Taking sole credit for ending the insurgency in Punjab, he fashioned himself as an antiterrorism and security expert and authority figure, even as he enacted and embodied a violent masculinity in responding to security challenges with characteristic repression. He became something of a complicated figure, appreciated by the government for what he did in Punjab, but seen as a sexual harasser as well because of a famous charge brought against him by a high-ranking civil servant for assaulting her at a party.[45] He was represented as both the uncouth Jat and a "supercop" (a sobriquet used in the Indian news media). Many in the Sikh community vilified him, though not as much for the sexual scandal, but for his violent tactics of policing.[46] He had served for over two decades in Assam, another border region of unrest, where, as inspector general of police, he became well known for his use of counterinsurgent violence that some Indian journalists praised by calling it "no-nonsense."[47] At the end of his career, he returned to Assam as a "security adviser," a position that rankled many in the region who had been critical of his tactics.[48] During the insurgency of the Tamil Tigers in Sri Lanka, the Sri Lankan government used him as a "security adviser," as did Narendra Modi in Gujarat after the pogrom of the Muslims in 2002. After the "success" in Punjab, others in the fields of security came to call his counterinsurgency tactics the "Gill Doctrine."[49] While this honorific was considered a testament to his contributions to the police force, the doctrine itself is far from his individual invention; instead, Gill is both a beneficiary as well as a product of the security regime, one that became central to the postcolonial security state trying to maintain its colonially endowed territory. Securitized responses to internal threats, that focus on raw state coercion and the co-optation of minority identities and of border communities, have emerged from the history of the colonial and the counterinsurgent state[50] and continue to be widely deployed across the South Asian subcontinent.[51]

At the height of the state's counterinsurgency campaign in 1992, Gill's tenure as the director general of police was supplemented by Beant Singh's election as chief minister. Singh was a rural politician who had moved up the ranks and publicly ordered his local political appointees to not interfere with police operations. Gill incorporated the historical and militaristic representation of Sikh warrior masculinity into the police, while remaining a favorite guest of the members of the English press.[52] Together, Gill and Singh created a public image of law and order that was designed to resonate with a large section of the rural and urban Sikh community and matched well with the dominant political culture of rural Punjab. Chima notes that governmental and administrative officers regularly complained that they felt subservient to the police, but these complaints fell on deaf ears as long as a staunchly loyal Beant Singh was in power.[53]

Gill's masculinity, in service of the nation, turned Punjab not only into a target of police or military operations, but into what was widely termed a "hot spot" of terrorism—enabling a securitizing of Punjab through a mode of control over particular spaces that we now see in many other parts of India and the world. As an important member of the Jat Sikh community, he had kinship and government networks that hailed him in diverse ways: as the face of a repressive state in border regions, he was seen as the rescuer of the state and the nation. However, importantly, he moved from a policeman, in police institutions that were little changed from its colonial "public order" rule[54] to a more recent version: the security expert who was now transforming policing into a securitizing force. He claimed that he was securitizing the region through better information gathering and networking, while opposing the power of other elite civil servants, recalcitrant politicians, or preceding police chiefs. In sum, his argument was that democratically elected representatives and elite bureaucrats (which had continuities with colonial civil service) could not be allowed to interfere in the security project.

This shift to a powerful male security expert is visible in his writings. In an article entitled "Endgame in Punjab: 1988–1993," Gill writes of the changes that he brought (and takes credit for) to the police to fight what he calls "terrorism" in Punjab. He writes, "The movement for the creation of Khalistan was one of the most virulent terrorist campaigns in the world."[55] Rather than political solutions that he views as an "appeasement of terrorists," he claims he did something new and radical, creating "counter-terrorist and counter-insurgency operations in Punjab that also challenged established traditions of response to situations of extreme and widespread militancy." He goes on to claim that rather than using armed violence, he used new security methods, asserting that the "defeat of terrorism" was "unambiguously the result of the counter-terrorist measures implemented in the state by the security forces."[56] These include replacing older weapons with more military style weapons for the police; increasing the size of the police force from twenty-five thousand men to sixty thousand; creating greater integration and coordination between the army and the police; and collecting, analyzing, and sharing information across these forces. From the localized practices of the police, he claims that he created a shift toward an information network of security forces—a more network-centric approach. Thus, Gill states that "successful counter-terrorist are based on accurate and detailed intelligence on terrorist networks and activities," in which even the local police station needs to become incorporated into the security framework. Each police station, he writes, is identified and categorized, a "village-wise analysis" is carried out to understand their relationship with insurgents, patterns are found pertaining to sources and flows of weapons, and intelligence is found by interrogation and infiltration. Gill states that he created "a large body of corroborated data based on surveillance operations, informers, interrogations and the progressive infiltration of many of the terrorist gangs." He continues by claiming that by "early 1989 itself, a fairly clear, accurate and continuously updated picture was available on the jurisdiction, membership, activities, strategies and networks of each of the major gangs operating in the state." Gill speaks of the need to overcome bureaucratic infighting and turf battles and inept and corrupt politicians, as well as government policies at both the central and the state levels that he deems "confused, irresponsible and ill-informed."[57]

Several aspects of this description of securitization are worth mentioning. First, he designates the insurgents as criminals as well as terrorists so that both police and military securitization become necessary to contain these groups. Second, by redirecting the source of violence as caused by terrorists, he claims that he was able to control the population. Third, using his position as a powerful Jat Sikh, he argues that this insurgency was a caste insurgency of an "oligarchy," an "ethnic cluster" that did not represent Sikh interests and had no resonance with other groups.[58] He redesignates human rights activists as "terrorist front organizations" and argues that it was only policing and securitizing, rather than political negotiations, that would end the conflict.

Despite this narrative of securitizing through improved techniques of intelligence gathering and surveillance, it was some more old-fashioned practices of police—ones that had their roots in the colonial state[59]—that created a state of terror among the population and led to killings of many journalists, human rights workers, and ordinary people. Under Gill, the police and security forces seemed to be everywhere, in villages as in towns and cities, and at every major street corner, embodying a threat of violence that could randomly erupt at any time or place. They could detain anyone, and did so, targeting especially young men in rural areas. They killed with impunity, used extortion, and tortured and sexually abused detainees (and the law allowed them to detain without habeas corpus). At the same time, those policemen seen as insubordinate or protesting at the injustice of police, as well as whistleblowers within the security apparatus, were subjected to torture and harassment in the form of false legal cases.[60] Police surveillance of people in villages extended to entering homes and arresting people at will, since the emergency laws passed by the government gave them immense power to arrest and detain people without evidence of a crime being committed. Gill created a special force, known as Black Cats—militants turned undercover police agents—that provided information about insurgent identities.[61] Many people we interviewed told us tragic stories, whether of children killed by police, women sexually assaulted, relatives in the police who were targeted by their fellows, or young men who had to leave the country to escape being killed.

Our fieldwork revealed that decades later, many believed that the brutality of the counterinsurgency had led to the migration, drug epidemics, and the abysmal economic conditions that they saw in the present. Many in the region continued to see Gill as a traitor to the Sikh community and one who not only encouraged but also actively enabled state violence at all levels of the security apparatus.[62] While many did express relief at the end of police violence and civilian deaths under the regime of state counterinsurgent repression of insurgency, most did not see the police as saviors—they understood that one kind of violence had been repressed by another kind of violence. They also challenged the notion that all insurgents were terrorists, seeing them as husbands, brothers, and sons, economic, familial, traumatized, or community subjects rather than criminals. As much as our interlocutors blamed the insurgency, they also blamed the government counterinsurgent program for its violence and its appropriation of local kinship networks to recruit coethnics into the Punjab police, which served to draw "battle-lines within the villages, with Sikh fighting Sikh, and the police backing their 'good guys.'"[63]

Through our interviews with police officers who had been part of the counterinsurgency, what became visible was the extent to which securitization came to encompass civil society, as governance was taken over by the police. In a conversation with one particular police officer, we learned that civil governance had given way to police control and rule by security forces—though this officer believed that such governance was helpful. What emerged was a picture of police as government and governance as securitizing. This officer remembered that "most of the judiciary in the districts and subdivisions, they were nonfunctional," and "even police officers who did some atrocities, they also worked really hard to maintain the peace." He went on to relay,

> We were deciding marital disputes—everything. People were coming to us, restoring girls back with honor to their in-laws' house. And if separation had to be done, we were making sure that they had enough for their life. For these kinds of disputes, civil in nature, and also land disputes, this also gave opportunity for corrupt officers to make money. The magistracy did not fill the duties, so the police had to fill the vacuum. Police had to even do things like sit in examination halls in schools to make sure that people weren't cheating. . . . So many normal activities were held. Film star nights were organized by the police.

This governance relied on a paternalist form of securitizing of the region and community, where police saw themselves as peacemakers, as producing harmony and negotiating communal strife in the region, rather than as responsible for violence. The widespread extrajudicial killings were seen as the work of a few "bad apples," instead of as a more systemic pattern of policing. This paternalism of the police also stands in stark contrast to narratives from earlier phases of the conflict, where locals expected militants to arbitrate the same village-level disputes, while the local police was viewed as too unprepared, poorly trained, and corrupt to adequately react to insurgent violence.[64] It was clear from this interview that it was not just the insurgency that had become securitized, but the entire population as well.

Paternalism and the Demonization of Sikhs as National Threat

While securitizing transformed the colonial "martial race" and the postcolonial "soldier" into the "security expert," for those Sikh men not in the police or military, there were few ways to inhabit patriarchy that did not expose them to state violence. For some Sikh men we spoke with, even those belonging to the dominant Jat caste, the loss of a notion of masculine protector in the familial form, as protective paternalism, came as a blow since they could neither be the militant, the security operative, the baptized Sikh who became the target of the police, nor even the soldier-protector of the Indian nation. While historical military tradition had enabled Sikh males to see themselves as the protectors of the nation, the insurgency transformed them into the figures of the terrorist and the extremist. Those whom we interviewed were highly aware of these shifts, sorrowfully cognizant that they had been demonized no matter which class, region, caste, or community they belonged to. The Indian nation now considered them all as "terrorists." As Gurmeet, now retired after civil service, told us, "People used to feel safe with a Sikh. In a bus, they would say that a Sikh is sitting there, go sit with him. And now they are doing this to us?"

Gurmeet mentioned that he had also been very hurt by the behavior of those he served and worked with all over India, and who now began to see him as a threat to the country and began to harass him at work. He felt that there was a religious divide between the rest of India and the Sikhs that had not been present in the secular past of postindependence India:

> Earlier, I never thought of my religion, but I felt after that [period] I was being identified as a Sikh officer, . . . that there was some incident that happened after that, there were so many complaints against me—they filed so many complaints against me accusing me of being a criminal-minded officer that is favoring the Sikhs, that I am anti-Hindu, and that I am harboring the extremists. . . . Yes, yes, they found the excuse to call me criminal-minded and all that.

Targeted as a sympathizer with the "militants" and "terrorists," such that he spent a great deal of his time defending himself and his work, Gurmeet retired with great bitterness about how he had been treated, seeing such treatment as having long-term effects on Sikhs' loyalty to the nation. Using the language of "alienation" from the Indian nation, he went on to say the following, with much sadness and sorrow in his voice:

> The anti-Sikh riots and Bluestar made the Sikhs alienated. They felt that this was not their country, the country we fought for all the time: World War I, World War II, the independence movement, Bhagat Singh, suffering in the Partition. The wars with Pakistan and China. We have done this for the country. We have gone to the highest peaks, into Sri Lanka, and the deserts of Rajasthan. Our community is the largest provider of soldiers to this country, farmers, transporters, etc. . . . And now they are doing this to us? So, people started thinking of leaving the country. This migration to Canada and a big wave started after this. Before that Canada was nowhere in the picture. Before '47, everyone was going to the UK; after '47, again to the UK. Roughly after '60, more went to the US.

As a member of the all-India civil service, Gurmeet had served all over the country and had seen himself as central to the making of the Indian nation through his service. For many like him, military service for his parents' and grandparents' generation, and civil service for him, had been not just a means of social mobility or evidence of a colonial construct of masculinity, but also came from allegiance to Indian nationalism in the decades after independence that promised "unity in diversity." Allegations of disloyalty to the nation thus hit hard at his own sense of loyal soldierly service that he had inherited from the family and which he had taken into civil service. Such shifts in attitudes also explained why some Sikh men became more religiously observant, moving their loyalty to the community instead of to the nation. Lawyer and activist Mallika Kaur's interviews, for instance, make this comparison: "In the 1970s it was very difficult to find in our university any student who was an *Amritdhari* [baptized in the religion]—not fashionable. But now, after 1984 Operation Bluestar, it suddenly became the opposite, it became very unusual to find persons who would not have a flowing beard and saffron [the color of sacrifice in the Sikh ethos] turban."[65] Kaur's research on attitudes of young men resonates with our project in an effort to address the demonization of Sikhs as a threat. As our work reveals, the splintering of masculinities during this period produced a complex set of responses that reconfigured gender both during and after the insurgency.

Conclusion

The official calculation of "peace" and "success" in repressing the insurgency hides the many disturbances that unsettled the postcolonial state. Two causes of this unsettling are the social changes enabled by altered masculinities and the reassertion of patriarchal power by the state and the insurgency. To the extent that the designation of Sikhs as terrorists and militants in India and transnationally has now moved to Muslim bodies, enabled by a new Hindu nationalism and an American "war on terror" with its global security regime, Sikh males are now being recuperated in new ways: as migrants, as unemployed youth, or as bodies riddled with drugs or cancers.[66] As biometric identity cards and digital surveillance transform policing and power,[67] the entire country is being securitized using the same regime tactics that enabled Gill's controversial doctrine. The new Hindu nationalism's targets are now both those border states and those seen as "antinationalists" within it: journalists, activists, women advocating for their rights, Muslims, Dalits, Adivasis, farmers. Colonial laws of sedition are being repurposed for repression, and state counterinsurgencies remain to exercise violence to protect the postcolonial security state.

These contemporary iterations of state masculinities have continuities with the conflicts of the 1980s as well as with the history of the colonial state's military and its celebration of Jat Sikh warrior masculinity. The violence of the counterinsurgency in Punjab continues into the present even twenty-five years later, not just in material but in affective ways, through precarities of health and employment, the ruthless targeting of political dissent, and the worsening economy of the region. Suicides by both farmers and agricultural labor have risen,[68] as rural indebtedness and disinvestment by the Central Government in New Delhi and neoliberal policies to corporatize agriculture in the state have led to protests by farmers that began in October 2020 and continued for over a year.[69] Caste patriarchies remain powerful[70] even as Dalit groups have improved their standing through remittances from migration. As the postcolonial state repurposes the American war on terror to designate non-Hindus as threatening Others to the Indian nation, the designation of protest—especially in border states across the North—as terrorism enables securitizing the region through colonial and postcolonial laws, military and paramilitary presence, and targeting of communities in gendered ways. Rural areas are under new forms of repression and threat by a state intent on privatizing even more domains of state control and to enable capitalist extraction. The ways in which emerging forms of resistance—such as the farmers' protest—can undo the security mechanisms of the postcolonial state remains to be seen.

Inderpal Grewal is professor emerita in the Program in Women's, Gender, and Sexuality Studies at Yale University. She is a theorist of transnational feminism, focusing on imperialism, culture, and postcoloniality. The author and coeditor of many articles and several books and monographs, most recently *Saving the Security State: Exceptional Citizens in Twenty-First-Century America* (2017), she is currently working on projects addressing security regimes in the Global South, the resurgence of patriarchal authoritarian governments and anti-Muslim violence in India, and on masculinity and bureaucracy.

Dipin Kaur is a PhD candidate in the Department of Political Science at Yale University.

Sasha Sabherwal is the chancellor's postdoctoral fellow in the Department of Asian American Studies at the University of Illinois Urbana-Champaign.

Notes

We would like to thank those who helped and hosted us, and all those who took the time to talk about some painful memories that they would rather forget. We are so appreciative of all those who shared that past. We would also like to thank Sahana Ghosh, Samar Al-Bulushi, and anonymous reviewers for their thoughtful comments. We are grateful for the feedback from the Workshop on Religion, Gender, and the Politics of Security, as well as the Punjab Reading Group, in particular Anshu Malhotra, Harjant Gill, and Mauricio Najarro. We would like to thank the Luce Foundation and Toby Volkmann for supporting our research in Punjab.

1. See, e.g., G. Singh, *Ethnic Conflict in India*. See also G. Singh and Kim, "Limits of India's Ethno-linguistic Federation."

2. See Gossman, "India's Secret Armies"; Fair, "Lessons from India's Experience"; Chima," Punjab Police and Counterinsurgency"; Hultquist, "Countering Khalistan."

3. See Puri, Judge, and Sekhon, *Terrorism in Punjab*; Dhillon, *Identity and Survival*; J. Grewal and Banga, *Punjab in Prosperity and Violence*; Shani, *Sikh Nationalism and Identity*; Rajinder Kaur, *Sikh Identity and National Integration*.

4. J. Kaur and Dhami, "Protecting the Killers." See also Mukhoty and Kothari, *Who Are the Guilty?*; Silva, Marwaha, and Klingner, *Violent Deaths and Enforced Disappearances*.

5. In another article, we have discussed how women responded to and remembered the conflict and the ways that it altered their notions of gender, family, and community. See I. Grewal and Sabherwal, "Slow Violence."

6. See, e.g., Mahmood, "Sikhs in Canada"; G. Singh and Tatla, *Sikhs in Britain*.

7. H. Gill, "Transnational Hair (and Turban)."

8. Axel, *Nation's Tortured Body*; Shani, "Memorialization of Ghallughara."

9. Dagar and Kumar, *Victims of Militancy*.

10. Even though in this article we emphasize the period beginning June 1984, Prime Minister Indira Gandhi's project of Sikh control started with the dismantling of Sikh opposition to the undemocratic national emergency she imposed beginning in 1975. Gandhi remained deeply contradictory in her own politics—spearheading a campaign to dismantle local Sikh leadership, yet relying on their warrior masculinity by deploying them as bodyguards for her personal protection. See Tully and Jacob, *Amritsar*, 10, 57.

11. I. Grewal and Sabherwal, "Slow Violence."

12. See Kumar et al., "Reduced to Ashes"; Amnesty International, *Human Rights Violations in the Punjab*; J. Kaur and Dhami, "Protecting the Killers."

13. Butalia, *Other Side of Silence*; Das, *Life and Words*.

14. See A. Gupta, *Red Tape*.

15. See Jakobsh, *Relocating Gender in Sikh History*.

16. See Oberoi, *Construction of Religious Boundaries*.

17. H. Gill, "Transnational Hair (and Turban)"; H. Gill, "Masculinity, Mobility and Transformation."

18. Dhavan, *When Sparrows Became Hawks*.

19. See Choudhry, "Militarized Masculinities," 713–50; Cohen, "Military and Indian Democracy."

20. See Imy, *Faithful Fighters*; Streets, *Martial Races*; Sinha, *Colonial Masculinity*.

21. Mann, "Media Framing."

22. See Wilkinson, *Army and Nation*.

23. Sikhs constitute less than 60 percent of the population of postpartition Punjab. While the recruitment and securitization of other Punjabi communities is important, it is outside the scope of our study given Sikhs' unique position as the prime targets of both state violence and counterinsurgent recruitment in this period.

24. The site, located in Amritsar, Punjab, is better known as the Darbar Sahib, Harmandir Sahib, or Golden Temple.

25. In response to Operation Bluestar, over two thousand Sikh Army men from all over the country attacked, mutinied, and deserted en masse. See Kundu, "Indian Armed Forces." For records of the multiple direct disciplinary infractions by Sikhs in the army in June 1984, see Tully and Jacob, *Amritsar*. See also Pettigrew, *The Sikhs of the Punjab*.

26. Although non-Sikhs—General A. S. Vaidya (India's chief of army staff) and Lieutenant General K. Sundarji—were in charge of the deployment of the army in Punjab, Operation Bluestar was planned and led by two Sikh men: Lieutenant General Ranjti Singh Dayal and Major General K. S. Brar. See Tully and Jacob, *Amritsar*. General Vaidya was assassinated in 1986 by the insurgent Khalistan Commando Force in retaliation for his involvement. See Mahmood, *Fighting for Faith and Nation*.

27. The insurgent defense of the temple complex was led by two retired Sikh major generals, Shahbeg Singh and Jaswant Singh Bhullar, who had other ex-army men under their command. See Wilkinson, *Army and Nation*, 150.

28. Chima, "Punjab Police and Counterinsurgency," 271–75.

29. Mark Tully and Satish Jacob catalogue how Bhindranwale was initially encouraged by the Congress Party, where Sanjay Gandhi and Zail Singh both used him to increase the party's power in Punjab over that of the Akali Dal (a Sikh regional party). See Tully and Jacob, *Amritsar*, 60–65. See also Nayar and Singh, *Tragedy of Punjab*.

30. *Financial Express*, "KPS Gill Dead." See also Sahni, *Fragility of Order*; Bal, "Lessons Not Learnt."

31. Deras constitute sectarian communities that belong to the long tradition of local saints and preachers that dot the region and exist mostly outside the framework of the orthodox religious establishments. While deras are powerful centers of power that can combine political and religious authority, they are often ignored in a great deal of research on politics in South Asia, though not ignored by political parties.

32. Oberoi, *Construction of Religious Boundaries*.

33. Videos of Bhindranwale's speeches are available on YouTube. See Bhindranwale, "Under What Law?"; Bhindranwale, "Historic Moments."

34. Tatla, "Unbearable Lightness."

35. Pritam Singh and Purewal, "Resurgence of Bhindranwale's Image."

36. I. Grewal and Sabherwal, "Slow Violence."

37. One might argue that it was not Bhindranwale but the central government's attack (Operation Bluestar) on the Golden Temple, which Bhindranwale had occupied, that united Sikhs across castes and across its diasporas against Indira Gandhi, then prime minister.

38. Mir, *Social Space of Language*; Bigelow, "Post-partition Pluralism."

39. This fieldwork comprised three summers of research between 2015 and 2018 and semistructured interviews with thirty people from across the state, men and women of different castes in the districts of Ludhiana, Amritsar, Bhatinda, Patiala, and Rupnagar.

40. I. Grewal and Sabherwal, "Slow Violence."

41. I. Grewal and Sabherwal, "Slow Violence."

42. M. Kaur, *Faith, Gender, and Activism in the Punjab Conflict*.

43. Chima, "Punjab Police and Counterinsurgency."

44. *Financial Express*, "KPS Gill Dead." See also Sahni, "Fragility of Order"; Bal, "Lessons Not Learnt."

45. I. Grewal, "Civil Servant and the Supercop."

46. Ghuman, *Punjab da Butcher*.

47. Karmakar, "KPS Gill."

48. Karmakar, "KPS Gill."

49. Mahadevan, "Gill Doctrine."

50. For instance, the colonial army in India also recruited heavily from the Jat Sikh population, especially those based in rural areas, for its external security needs

during the two world wars. International recruitment provided recruits avenues for emigration, and remittances from soldiers overseas enhanced Punjab's economic fortunes. See Mazumder, *Indian Army*; Tatla, "Sikh Free and Military Migration."

51. Staniland, "Counterinsurgency Is a Bloody, Costly Business."

52. Chima, "Punjab Police and Counterinsurgency."

53. Chima, "Punjab Police and Counterinsurgency," 271.

54. Kalhan et al., "Colonial Continuities."

55. K. P. S. Gill, "Endgame in Punjab."

56. K. P. S. Gill, "Endgame in Punjab."

57. K. P. S. Gill, "Endgame in Punjab."

58. This view has since been replicated in academic work on the subject. See G. Singh, *Ethnic Conflict in India*.

59. Sauli, "Circulation and Authority."

60. Ensaaf, "Last Killing."

61. Mahadevan, "Counter Terrorism in the Indian Punjab"; Fair, "Lessons from India's Experience."

62. Gossman, *Dead Silence*; G. Singh, *Ethnic Conflict in India*.

63. Gupta and Sandhu, "True Grit."

64. Fair, "Lessons from India's Experience."

65. M. Kaur, *Faith, Gender, and Activism*, 184.

66. See, e.g., *Udta Punjab* (dir. Abhishek Chaubey, 2016)—though there is much debate about the impacts of this film as enabling new kinds of securitized control over youth in Punjab.

67. The impacts of these new biometric surveillance regimes on gender issues is an important area of research. See Kelkar et al., *Aadhaar*.

68. Singh, Bhangoo, and Sharma, *Agrarian Distress*.

69. See, e.g., Ravinder Kaur, "How a Farmers' Protest"; N. Gill, "Popular Upsurge"; M. Kaur, "Unprecedented Farmers Protests." As we submit this essay, the Modi government seems to have caved to the demands of the protestors and has agreed to repeal the laws—especially because of upcoming elections in Punjab and Uttar Pradesh, two states where powerful Jat farmers were part of the protest.

70. P. Singh and Shemyakina, "Gender-Differential Effects."

References

Amnesty International. "Human Rights Violations in Punjab: Use and Abuse of the Law." Amnesty International. Index Number ASA 20/011/1991. May 9, 1991.

Axel, Brian Keith. *The Nation's Tortured Body: Violence, Representation, and the Formation of a Sikh "Diaspora."* Durham, NC: Duke University Press, 2001.

Bal, Hartosh Singh. "Lessons Not Learnt: The Left and Right Have Distorted KPS Gill's Success against Terrorism." *Scroll.in*, July 9, 2017. https://scroll.in/article/842699/lessons-not-learnt-the-left-and-right-have-distorted-kps-gills-success-against-terrorism.

Bigelow, Anna. "Post-partition Pluralism: Placing Islam in Indian Punjab." In *Punjab Reconsidered: History, Culture, and Practice*, edited by Anshu Malhotra and Farina Mir, 409–34. New Delhi: Oxford University Press, 2012.

Bhindranwale, Jarnail Singh. "Historic Moments—Rare Speeches of Saint Jarnail Singhji Bhindranwale 1984 Historic Moments." Part 6. YouTube video, 29:38. Uploaded by Punjabi Entertainment, October 3, 2015. https://www.youtube.com/watch?v=t7FYKnXwivk.

Bhindranwale, Jarnail Singh. "Under What Law Were Our Buses Set Alight?—

Saint Bhindranwale: Saka Chando Kalan (14.9.1981)." YouTube video, 5:43. Uploaded by JagowaleTV, September 13, 2017. https://www.youtube.com/watch ?v=BNTftGCGkpw.

Butalia, Urvashi, *The Other Side of Silence: Voices from the Partition of India*. Durham, NC: Duke University Press, 2000.

Chima, Jugdep. "The Punjab Police and Counterinsurgency against Sikh Militants in India: The Successful Convergence of Interests, Identities, and Institutions." In *Policing Insurgencies: Cops as Counterinsurgents*, edited by C. Christine Fair and Sumit Ganguly, 258–90. Oxford: Oxford University Press, 2014.

Choudhry, Prem. "Militarized Masculinities: Shaped and Reshaped in Colonial South-East Punjab." *Modern Asian Studies* 47, no. 3 (2013): 713–50.

Cohen, Stephen P. "The Military and Indian Democracy." In *India's Democracy: An Analysis of Changing State-Society Relations*, edited by Atul Kohli, 99–143. Princeton, NJ: Princeton University Press, 1988.

Dagar, Rainuka, Pramod Kumar and Neerja. *Victims of Militancy: Punjab*. Chandigarh: Institute for Development and Communication, 2001.

Das, Veena. *Life and Words: Violence and the Descent into the Ordinary*. Berkeley: University of California Press, 2006.

Dhavan, Purnima. *When Sparrows Became Hawks: The Making of the Sikh Warrior Tradition, 1699–1799*. Oxford: Oxford University Press, 2011.

Dhillon, Kirpal. *Identity and Survival: Sikh Militancy in India, 1978–1993*. Delhi: Penguin India, 2006.

Ensaaf. "The Last Killing." YouTube video, 23:01. Uploaded May 23, 2014. https:// www.youtube.com/watch?v=bKmxqqhlPD0.

Fair, C. Christine. "Lessons from India's Experience in the Punjab, 1978–1993." In *India and Counterinsurgency: Lessons Learned*, edited by Sumit Ganguly and David P. Fidler, 107–26. London: Routledge, 2009.

Financial Express. "KPS Gill Dead at Eighty-Two: Ten Things to Know about the 'Supercop' Who Uprooted Militancy in Punjab." May 26, 2017. https:// www.financialexpress.com/india-news/former-punjab-dgp-kps-gill-dead-at -82-10-things-to-know-about-the-supercop-who-uprooted-militancy/687609/.

Ghuman, Sarbjit Singh. *Punjab da Butcher KPS Gill (KPS Gill—The Butcher of Punjab)*. Amritsar: Fatehnama, 2019.

Gill, Harjant S. "Masculinity, Mobility, and Transformation in Punjabi Cinema: From *Putt Jattan De (Sons of Jat Farmers)* to *Munde UK De (Boys of UK)*." *South Asian Popular Culture* 10, no. 2 (2012): 109–22.

Gill, Harjant S. "Transnational Hair (and Turban): Sikh Masculinity, Embodied Practices, and Politics of Representation in an Era of Global Travel." *Ethnography*. Published ahead of print, May 4, 2020. https://doi.org/10.1177 /1466138120923712.

Gill, K. P. S. "Endgame in Punjab: 1988–1993." *Faultlines* 1, no. 1 (1999). https:// www.satp.org/satporgtp/publication/faultlines/volume1/fault1-kpstext.htm.

Gill, Navyug. "A Popular Upsurge against Neoliberal Arithmetic in India." *Al Jazeera*, December 11, 2020. https://www.aljazeera.com/opinions/2020/12/11/a -popular-upsurge-against-neoliberal-arithmetic-in-india.

Gossman, Patricia. "Dead Silence: The Legacy of Human Rights Abuses in Punjab." Human Rights Watch and Physicians for Human Rights, May 1994. https:// www.hrw.org/reports/India0594.pdf.

Gossman, Patricia. "India's Secret Armies." In *Death Squads in Global Perspective: Murder with Deniability*, edited by Bruce B. Campbell and Arthur D. Brenner, 261–86. New York: Palgrave Macmillan, 2000.

Grewal, Inderpal. "The Civil Servant and the Supercop: Modesty, Security, and the State in Punjab." In *Punjabi Century*, edited by Anshu Malhotra. Hyderabad: Orient BlackSwan India, forthcoming.

Grewal, Inderpal, and Sasha Sabherwal. "Slow Violence in Post-1984 Punjab: Remembering, Forgetting, and Refusals." *Sikh Formations* 15, nos. 3–4 (2019): 343–60.

Grewal, J. S., and Indu Banga. *Punjab in Prosperity and Violence*. Chandigarh: K K Publishers and Institute for Punjab Studies, 1998.

Gupta, Akhil. *Red Tape: Bureaucracy, Structural Violence, and Poverty in India*. Durham, NC: Duke University Press, 2012.

Gupta, Shekhar, and Kanwar Sandhu. "Police Chief K. P. S. Gill Turns the Tide in Punjab with Controversial and Ruthless Methods." *India Today*, April 15, 1993.

Hultquist, Philip. "Countering Khalistan: Understanding India's Counter-Rebellion Strategies during the Punjab Crisis." *Journal of Punjab Studies* 22, no. 1 (2015): 93–121.

Imy, Kate. *Faithful Fighters: Identity and Power in the British Indian Army*. Stanford, CA: Stanford University Press, 2019.

Jakobsh, Doris. *Relocating Gender in Sikh History*. New Delhi: Oxford University Press, 2003.

Kalhan, Anil, Gerald P. Conroy, Mamta Kaushal, and Sam Scott Miller. "Colonial Continuities: Human Rights, Terrorism, and Security Laws in India." *Columbia Journal of Asian Law* 20, no. 1 (2006): 93–234.

Karmakar, Rahul. "KPS Gill: A 'Fearsome' Police Officer Even during Assam Agitation Days." *Hindustan Times*, May 27, 2017. https://www.hindustantimes.com/india-news/kps-gill-a-fearsome-police-officer-even-during-assam-agitation-days/story-BK0fPtNzIbjvBwqygvTvyH.html.

Kaur, Jaskaran, and Sukhman Dhami. "Protecting the Killers: A Policy of Impunity in Punjab, India." Human Rights Watch, October 17, 2007. https://www.hrw.org/sites/default/files/reports/india1007webwcover.pdf.

Kaur, Mallika. *Faith, Gender, and Activism in the Punjab Conflict: The Wheat Fields Still Whisper*. New York: Palgrave Macmillan, 2019.

Kaur, Mallika. "Unprecedented Farmers Protests in India: Lest We Miss This Feminist Moment." *Ms.*, December 10, 2020. https://msmagazine.com/2020/12/10/india-farmer-protest-feminist-women/.

Kaur, Rajinder. *Sikh Identity and National Integration*. Delhi: Intellectual, 1992.

Kaur, Ravinder. "How a Farmers' Protest in India Evolved into a Mass Movement That Refuses to Fade." *New Statesman*, February 19, 2021. https://www.newstatesman.com/international/2021/02/how-farmers-protest-india-evolved-mass-movement-refuses-fade.

Kelkar, Govind, et al. *Aadhaar: Gender, Identity and Development*. New Delhi: Academic Foundation, 2015.

Kumar, Ram Narayan, et al. "Reduced to Ashes: The Insurgency and Human Rights in Punjab." Kathmandu: South Asia Forum for Human Rights, 2003.

Kundu, Apurba. "The Indian Armed Forces' Sikh and Non-Sikh Officers' Opinions of Operation Blue Star." *Pacific Affairs* 67, no. 1 (1994): 46–69.

Mahadevan, Prem. "Counter Terrorism in the Indian Punjab: Assessing the 'Cat' System." *Faultlines*, no. 18 (2007): 19–54.

Mahadevan, Prem. "The Gill Doctrine: A Model for Twenty-First Century Counter-terrorism?" *Faultlines*, no. 19 (2008). https://www.satp.org/satporgtp/publication/faultlines/volume19/Article1.htm.

Mahmood, Cynthia Keppley. *Fighting for Faith and Nation: Dialogues with Sikh Militants*. Philadelphia: University of Pennsylvania Press, 1996.

Mann, Richard D. "Media Framing and the Myth of Religious Violence: The Other-ing of Sikhs in *The Times of India*." *Sikh Formations* 12, no. 2–3 (2016): 120–41.

Mazumder, Rajit K. *The Indian Army and the Making of Punjab*. Delhi: Permanent Black, 2003.

Mir, Farina. *The Social Space of Language: Vernacular Culture in British Colonial Punjab*. Berkeley: University of California Press, 2010.

Mukhoty, Gobinda, and Rajni Kothari. *Who Are the Guilty?* Delhi: People's Union for Civil Liberties, 1984.

Nayar, Kuldip, and Khushwant Singh. *Tragedy Of Punjab: Operation Blue Star and After, with a New Postscript on Mrs. Gandhi's Assassination*. Delhi: Vision, 1985.

Oberoi, Harjot. *The Construction of Religious Boundaries: Culture, Identity, and Diversity in the Sikh Tradition*. Chicago: University of Chicago Press, 1994.

Puri, Haresh K., Paramjit S. Judge, and Jagrup Singh Sekhon. *Terrorism in Punjab: Understanding Grassroots Reality*. New Delhi: Har-Anand, 1999.

Sahni, Ajai. *The Fragility of Order: Essays in Honor of KPS Gill*. Delhi: Kautilya, 2019.

Sauli, Arnaud. "Circulation and Authority: Police, Public Space, and Territorial Control in Punjab, 1861–1920." In *Society and Circulation: Mobile People and Itinerant Cultures in South Asia, 1750–1950*, edited by Claude Markovits, Jacques Pouchepadass, and Sanjay Subrahmanyam, 215–39. Delhi: Permanent Black, 2003.

Shani, Giorgio. "The Memorialization of Ghallughara: Trauma, Nation, and Diaspora." *Sikh Formations* 6, no. 2 (2010): 177–92.

Shani, Giorgio. S*ikh Nationalism and Identity in a Global Age*. London: Routledge, 2009.

Silva, Romesh, Jasmine Marwaha, and Jeff Klingner. *Violent Deaths and Enforced Disappearances during the Counterinsurgency in Punjab, India: A Preliminary Quantitative Analysis*. Palo Alto, CA: Benetech's Human Rights Data Analysis Group and Ensaaf, 2009.

Singh, Gurharpal. *Ethnic Conflict in India: A Case-Study of Punjab*. Basingstoke, UK: Macmillan, 2000.

Singh, Gurharpal, and Heewon Kim. "The Limits of India's Ethno-linguistic Federation: Understanding the Demise of Sikh Nationalism." *Regional and Federal Studies* 28, no. 4 (2018): 427–45.

Singh, Gurharpal, and Darshan Singh Tatla. *Sikhs in Britain: The Making of a Community*. London: Zed, 2006.

Singh, Lakhwinder, Kesar Singh Bhangoo, and Rakesh Sharma. *Agrarian Distress and Farmer Suicides in North India*. Delhi: Routledge India, 2019.

Singh, Prakarsh, and Olga N. Shemyakina. "Gender-Differential Effects of Terrorism on Education: The Case of the 1981–1993 Punjab Insurgency." *Economics of Education Review*, no. 54 (2016): 185–210.

Singh, Pritam, and Navtej Purewal. "The Resurgence of Bhindranwale's Image in Contemporary Punjab." *Contemporary South Asia* 21, no. 2 (2013): 133–47.

Sinha, Mrinalini. *Colonial Masculinity: The "Manly Englishman" and the "Effeminate Bengali" in the Late Nineteenth Century*. Manchester: Manchester University Press, 2017.

Staniland, Paul. "Counterinsurgency Is a Bloody, Costly Business." *Foreign Policy*, November 24, 2009. https://foreignpolicy.com/2009/11/24/counterinsurgency-is-a-bloody-costly-business/.

Streets, Heather. *Martial Races: The Military, Race, and Masculinity in British Imperial Culture, 1857–1914*. Manchester: Manchester University Press, 2017.

Tatla, Darshan. "Sikh Free and Military Migration during the Colonial Period." In

The Cambridge Survey of World Migration, edited by Robin Cohen, 69–73. Cambridge: Cambridge University Press, 1995.

Tatla, Darshan. "The Unbearable Lightness of Diasporic Sikh Nationalism! From Anguished Cries of 'Khalistan' to Pleas for 'Recognition.'" *Sikh Formations* 8, no. 1 (2012): 59–85.

Tully, Mark, and Satish Jacob. *Amritsar: Mrs Gandhi's Last Battle*. Delhi: Rupa, 2006.

Wilkinson, Steven I. *Army and Nation: The Military and Indian Democracy since Independence*. Cambridge, MA: Harvard University Press, 2015.

Navigating the "Middle East" in Washington

Diasporic Experts and the Power
of Multiplicitous Diplomacy

Negar Razavi

Making my way into the lobby of the historic Willard Hotel in downtown Washington, DC—where the term "lobbying" is rumored to have originated—my eyes were drawn to the somber crowd of older white men, whose nearly matching dark suits clashed with the extravagant golds and crimsons of the hotel's opulent decor. Most of the men were huddled together in serious discussion, while several younger women cheerfully checked them in to the security conference that they were waiting to attend. A large banner behind the group revealed that the event was being hosted by a DC think tank notorious for its hawkish stance against Iran and which is bolstered by a wider neoconservative network known for its unwavering support of Israel's security interests within the nation's capital. When I had agreed to meet Jamshid,[1] an Iranian American foreign policy expert who works for another think tank, at the Willard that afternoon, I had not expected him to be attending a conference hosted by such a group, which has openly supported punitive sanctions, military interventions, and other forms of regime change against our native Iran.

My discomfort with this particular crowd must have been apparent, for when Jamshid finally approached me in the lobby, he quickly ushered the two of us away from the other conference attendees to sit in a far-removed corner of the lobby, all while smiling and making reassuring small talk. For the next hour, Jamshid continued to try to put me at ease, speaking openly in English about his life, his professional trajec-

Social Text 152 · Vol. 40, No. 3 · September 2022
DOI 10.1215/01642472-9771091   © 2022 Duke University Press

tory, and his work on Iran and the broader Middle East. He answered all my questions with funny anecdotes and simple, Tweetable assessments about the region, only occasionally breaking our easy flowing conversation to wave at someone from the conference milling about in the lobby between sessions. Finally, I felt emboldened enough to ask Jamshid what he thought about the think tank that organized this conference, given its hostile stance against Iran. His comforting, laid-back posture immediately changed. His reassuring smile, which had lingered all afternoon, instantly vanished. Looking over his shoulder to check where the rest of the conference goers were positioned, he switched to Persian for the first time that day:

> Look, I still have family in Iran. I don't like the Iranian regime of course, but I don't want to see America attack Iran [militarily]. I don't want to see Iran become Syria. . . . These guys [at the right-wing think tank] don't come out and say they want war with Iran, but when you close every possible door to negotiation, then that is what you are left with. Based on my conscience I cannot work for groups like this. Thankfully I don't need the money or the visibility. So, my conscience is clear.

Through this short interaction, Jamshid revealed how as a US-based policy expert with direct personal connections to the Middle East, he strategically navigates multiple (in this case, oppositional) transnational political networks to ensure his own influence in Washington. Thus, on the one hand, Jamshid has cultivated ties to a neoconservative think tank that counts among its supporters the most hardline defenders of Israel's security policies in Washington—even when such interests have directly contradicted US government priorities, as was the case with the Iran nuclear deal in 2015. Jamshid's willingness to engage this political faction, despite being from the very racialized community its members regularly vilify, speaks both to his ideological affinities but also his affective skills, which allow him political as well as social access to these circles. On the other hand, Jamshid made an effort to appeal to me, as a member of his own diasporic community critical of US empire. From the moment we met, he tried to settle my obvious anxieties about his own political commitments given his unexpected association with this problematic think tank. Later he stated his opposition to the group's more extreme, pro-war stances against Iran using his familial connections and drawing on nationalistic tropes ("not wanting to see Iran become Syria") to bolster his claims. Still, Jamshid took care not to have his critiques of the organization overheard by the other conference attendees by offering them in Persian—a language he knew none of his white counterparts spoke but that would further cement his affective connections to me. Meanwhile, he framed his decision not to take money from this think tank and its allies as a moral one, though, as I discovered later, the think tank he works for receives much of its funding from a donor that maintains a subtler though nonetheless antagonistic view of Iran.

Over the course of two years of ethnographic fieldwork in Washington DC studying the role of experts in shaping US security policies across the Middle East, I got to know a growing number of "diasporic experts"[2] like Jamshid, who use their personal ties to this region and its diasporas to exert their authority within US security debates. Like their white colleagues,[3] most of these experts work for think tanks and related policy research institutions that compete in what my interlocutors call the "marketplace of ideas"—the realm of elite debate that shapes US policy decisions abroad.[4] Within this competitive marketplace, I observed how these diasporic experts play a distinctive role given their connections (both real and perceived) to a region the United States has made its primary security target since 9/11.

My central assertion in this article is that experts like Jamshid are increasingly sought out in Washington not for their in-depth knowledge of the "Middle East" as a bounded geographic region "over there" but rather for their abilities to navigate and leverage competing relationships, funding sources, and political demands from the Middle East (and its diasporas) within the heart of the US empire. Their expertise, in other words, is enacted in their moving between and influencing different political networks, which circulate between the region and the United States, all while making the claims of one group meaningful or intelligible to another. In this way, a single expert can serve the interests of multiple stakeholders in Washington—from powerful Middle Eastern governments, to different segments of their own diasporic communities, to various factions within the white imperial security community. Jamshid was performing precisely this kind of affective, epistemological, and political labor that afternoon in the Willard; engaging in a form of diplomatic code-switching as he expertly moved from one person to another within the microcosm of the hotel lobby.

In their study of diplomatic representatives from British Overseas Territories, Fiona McConnell and Jason Dittmer contend that polities today are increasingly "multiplicities . . . existing in different states simultaneously. [Consequently] if polities are multiplicities, then the interactions between polities—their diplomacy—is also multiplicitous."[5] From my ethnographic research in Washington, I came to observe how the US empire itself operates as a multiplicitous, transnational polity, a point I will return to in a moment. In turn, I see the diasporic experts from the Middle East as performing a type of "multiplicitous diplomacy" among competing transnational networks, helping to circulate and legitimate different ideas about security as they move across political, geographic, and ideological boundaries.

Through this argument, I am first making a broader claim about how the US empire—and particularly Washington, as its proverbial center—operates in practice as a transnational site of exchange and circulation. Here I align with the scholarship of other critical anthropologists of empire,[6] who have used the people-centered tools of ethnography to further uncover the security logics, technologies, and actors that sustain US empire, with the express goal of challenging and ultimately "refusing" them.[7] Many of these studies have rightly pushed back against the spatial and temporal fixedness often attributed to the US empire, particularly as it relates to a global war on terror[8] that has been defined by its ability to be "both everywhere and nowhere."[9] For the most part, however, these insights have been gathered by studying the violent effects of the US empire as it expands globally or within its own sovereign boundaries through settler-colonialism. Those few scholars who have turned the ethnographic or historical lens on to the securitizing elites in Washington have focused almost entirely on the role of traditional US elites—presumed to be white male citizens who work for the highest ranks of the US military or government.[10] My research goes further in its analysis by revealing how a much wider field of elites outside the US government, including many from the Global South, compete to shape the US security imaginary from within Washington.

By drawing attention to the specific influence of elites from the Middle East and its diasporas in this contested security milieu, I am showing the extent to which this region exerts power over Washington, thus flipping persisting tropes advanced by both critics and supporters of US empire that treat the people and governments of the region as either passive targets of American hegemony or imperial proxies with little of their own strategic interests or influence. My findings align with recent calls from scholars of the Middle East and its diasporas to further destabilize the traditional geopolitical imaginaries and boundaries—rooted in earlier colonial, Orientalist projects—that continue to isolate the Middle East from global histories, circulations, and political-economic and security processes.[11] As Asef Bayat and Linda Herrera write in the introduction to *Global Middle East: Into to the Twenty-First Century,* "Today a powerful neo-Orientalist approach depicts the region as largely homogenous, closed, parochial, and resistant to change. Imagined in this fashion, the Middle East has little of value to offer to the world and is responsible for its own troubles."[12] Some of the leading voices pushing against these deeply entrenched geographic and epistemological boundaries are those who study the region's many diasporic communities. They trace the region through the memories, movements, traumas, and political claims of the people who have left it.[13] That is, these scholars show the extent to which "Iran" exists in Tehran as much as it does in Tehrangeles (Los Angeles's nickname as the home to the largest Iranian diasporic community).[14] In this article, I build on these important interventions by showing how elite actors from this globally defined Middle East—comprised of mobile diasporas, local and diverse communities, and regional governments—serve as important political interlocutors within Washington, helping to co-construct but also reimagine empire from its contested center.

Ultimately, the way that I methodologically observe and analyze these dynamics within Washington is through my ethnographic encounters with diasporic experts like Jamshid. This approach has given me unprecedented access to these particular political actors, while allowing me to better attend to the contradictions in their experiences and also the political, ethnic, and even ideological diversity that exists among them. As diasporic subjects, these analysts represent the full gamut of experiences of migration, exile, transnational movement, and multiple citizenships from across this diverse region.[15] They also hold various ideological positions vis-à-vis US empire. Some are overtly critical of US imperialism, while others align with the worst trope of the "native informant," who in the words of Hamid Dabashi "feign authority while telling their conquerors not what they need to know but what they want to hear."[16] This diversity is significant in understanding their role as multiplicitous diplomats, as each diasporic expert navigates and bolsters the security claims of different political networks and factions within DC.

Regardless of their actual backgrounds or views of US empire, meanwhile, these diasporic experts still operate within Washington as the racialized and religious "Other" in the post-9/11 logics of counterterror.[17] Their Otherness cuts in several contradictory directions that ultimately cement their unique role as multiplicitous diplomats within DC. Thus, their Otherness is increasingly recuperated as a kind of celebratory liberal understanding of diversity, which intentionally fails to challenge the core security and political-economic logics of the imperial apparatus.[18] At other times, these same personal entanglements shed doubt on these actors' perceived loyalties to the US empire. As anthropologist Amy Malek found in her study of Iranians in the diaspora, no matter how close such actors get to the US security state—including within the National Security Council itself—the state still fosters "continued suspicion of the allegiances and loyalties of dual nationals and concomitant security fears of espionage, terrorism, and treason."[19] These suspicions subsequently discipline these experts, removing their abilities to claim the same (albeit false) "objectivity" and expert authority of their white counterparts to comment and contribute to all security debates affecting the United States. However, these diasporic experts' Otherness is also what makes them strategically valuable within Washington's highly saturated marketplace of ideas. Only by understanding these contradictions can we see how these experts actually operate in Washington, rather than viewing them as simple tools of legitimation for an imagined monolithic, omnipotent US empire. To return to my core argument in this piece, we must instead view this minoritized group of experts as skilled diplomats who help create policy coherence among multiple, transnationally mobile actors from the Middle East who compete for power in Washington. In the remainder of this article, I will show how they enact this multiplicitous diplomacy in practice.

The Geopolitics of Funding in Washington

One of the most important ways these experts negotiate among various regional powers in Washington is by helping navigate what I term the "geopolitics of funding"—a specific site of contestation within DC's broader marketplace of ideas that implicates foreign states and their proxies in this city. In the context of US policy debates on the Middle East, regional governments—particularly from the Persian Gulf—have become some of the most dominant players in this geopolitics of funding.[20] According to a 2020 Center for International Policy (CIP) report, the United Arab Emirates (UAE) publicly donated $15.4 million to just six think tanks in DC from 2014 until 2018, while giving $20 million in a "secret" deal with the Middle East Institute in 2017.[21] The same report found that Qatar had given $8.5 million to several think tanks during this same period. And while the report could not track down the exact amount of Saudi contributions, the Gulf government was listed as a donor for at least four of the major foreign policy think tanks in DC.[22] Meanwhile, based on my own research, those think tanks more aligned ideologically with Israel, and particularly right-wing political factions within Israel, tend to get their funding from wealthy individual donors based in the United States, such as Haim Saban and Sheldon Adelson, or domestic interest groups like the American Israel Public Affairs Committee (AIPAC).[23] Regardless of whether this funding comes directly from foreign governments or indirectly through affiliated proxies in the United States, however, such financial power has allowed many of the rivalries and political dynamics of the region to permeate and ultimately shape the security debates in Washington. And while policy experts of all backgrounds have to grapple with the geopolitics of funding in DC, I would argue that the diasporic experts are more directly implicated because of their liminal status in Washington, representing different factions both within the region and the United States.

In some cases, diasporic experts use their in-betweenness to serve as direct sources of expertise on how to navigate the geopolitics of funding for their institutions. At one think tank that was coming under critical scrutiny for taking Gulf funding, Malek, an expert born and raised in the region, told me how his organization relied on him to court wealthy businessmen from Lebanon, Egypt, and other parts of the region (and the Arab diaspora) to help the organization better "diversify" their sources of funding and to further deflect criticism from other parts of the security policy community for taking so much Gulf funding. He was also regularly asked by the institution's leaders to sit in on their meeting with their regional donors, to act as a social mediator; putting the donors at ease, while translating many of the cultural and political nuances of the region for his white colleagues.

Other times, these diasporic experts become directly implicated in the geopolitical rivalries among donors, helping serve (sometimes inadvertently) different government stakeholders. For instance, Sayyed, an Egyptian American expert who worked for a think tank that takes significant funding from the United Arab Emirates, explained how he realized early on that their donors were particularly sensitive about any analysis produced in Washington that concerns the Muslim Brotherhood (MB), the Islamist political organization that operates in Egypt, Jordan, and several other Arab countries. Though Sayyed did not align ideologically with the MB, he wrote publicly against the mass imprisonment, killing, and torture of MB members by the Egyptian government in the aftermath of that country's 2013 military coup. Soon after he published these condemnations, Sayyed told me he started receiving messages from Emirati and Saudi government proxies in DC, accusing him of taking money from the MB. At one policy event, Sayyed ran into an acquaintance from another Gulf embassy who warned him that Emirati officials in DC were displeased with his writing on the MB and were voicing their concerns with other powerful figures in the city, including his bosses. He was not surprised, then, when his organization's leaders started taking a heavier editorial hand with his writings, couching their critiques in euphemisms about "being more objective" and "trying to offer the other perspective" on the issue—meaning the Egyptian government's official line defending their brutal crackdown. Nearly a year after we first met, I ran into Sayyed again. He had taken a new job at another organization known for its closer financial links to Qatar, which has historically supported the Muslim Brotherhood. Sayyed noted the irony that over time, he had been forced to increasingly ally himself with regional factions in DC that are more closely aligned with the MB, in essence reifying the accusations made against him. What he lamented most about his own experiences, however, was how effectively the donors (on all sides) had ultimately reduced the Egypt policy debate within Washington to a simplistic referendum on the Muslim Brotherhood. "There are so many more interesting and important questions that we should try to be answering about US policy [in Egypt]. Instead, they [the Gulf countries] are keeping us in DC preoccupied with the MB." Diasporic experts recounted similar issues relating to US policy toward Iran, Syria, Palestine, Turkey, and Yemen.

In a few cases, diasporic experts I met were forced to navigate these geopolitical dynamics as a way to even gain entry into the elite policy community of Washington. Michael, a Lebanese-born expert, recounted how after several rounds of interviews at a think tank, he was asked to attend a seemingly unrelated, off-the-record roundtable with other fellows from the organization, along with a board member, who is also a wealthy contributor to pro-Israeli groups in DC, and a pair of former Israeli government officials. Michael said that it became immediately clear that the purpose of this meeting was to gauge his views on Israel before they offered him the job—even though he was not going to be working on Israel directly. They wanted to ensure he was not overtly critical of the country and could engage this particular pro-Israel faction within Washington in ways they found ideologically palatable. Other diasporic experts shared comparable stories about institutions heavily funded by the Emiratis and Saudis.

Both Michael's and Sayyed's experiences demonstrate how regional powers have been able to use the geopolitics of funding to act out their own regional tensions within Washington. At the same time, their experiences speak to the overall disciplining effects that regional governments have on the nature and scope of policy debates in Washington through the geopolitics of funding, particularly as it (dis)affects diasporic experts. Through the pressures they exert on these experts as major donors to foreign policy think tanks, these governments have been able to demarcate the boundaries of what is possible in terms of US regional policy by determining who is recognized as a security expert, as was the case with Michael, or by reducing the complexities of regional issues to support their own security agendas, as Sayyed's story reveals. And while other scholars have more fully fleshed out the role of foreign funding in shaping the US foreign policy imaginary, especially among pro-Israeli voices in Washington,[24] my particular contribution here is to show how diasporic experts are increasingly on the front lines of this geopolitics of funding. Experts like Sayyed and Michael are brought into these think tanks, presumably to increase these institutions' diversity. But they are often forced (even before they are hired) to negotiate among competing governments and their powerful allies in Washington in order to legitimate their own positions and exert their influence.

Bringing the Middle East to Washington: Relationality and Affect across Borders

Diasporic experts further perform their role as multiplicitous diplomats within Washington by providing the US security community particular kinds of access to the Middle East through their personal relationships, affective ties, and experiences in the region.

I was often struck over my ten years studying and working with the DC-based policy community how despite the expansive reach of the US military, economic, and surveillance power across the Middle East (and beyond), its experts maintain surprisingly little contact with the societies they analyze on behalf of the US empire. Partly, these limitations can be explained by the widespread lack of linguistic fluency within these elite American security circles, which limit who they can speak to and study. However, the problem of access goes much deeper, as the majority of white regional experts in DC refuse to spend extended time in the Middle East. Even in countries like Egypt, Lebanon, or Jordan, which have been (for the most part) friendly places for members of the white security community to visit, work, and study, only a handful have spent more than a few weeks in these countries. Most travel to the region on short one- or two-week "research trips" or "fact-finding missions," sometimes as members of large formal delegations. Even then, as Bassem, an Egyptian expert in exile, explained, "Most people here [in DC] don't have the luxury to meet with Egyptians and talk to them in their own language. They have to hire a translator, or they don't even bother and only meet with English speaking elites. There is a kind of 'club' of Egyptians who the DC-based experts always speak to. . . . And these people [in Cairo] know English, and they have an agenda." Thus, much of the responsibility and labor of facilitating "access" to the region for the DC security expert community falls on the shoulders of diasporic experts and research assistants.

Most directly, these diasporic experts offer this regional access by facilitating meetings between their personal and professional networks in the region and those in the United States. During the 2011 Arab Spring uprisings, for instance, DC-based Egyptian and Egyptian American experts were in the unique position of connecting their friends and family members actively protesting in Tahrir to think-tank experts in Washington, along with US government officials, who had few other means of contacting these previously unknown activists. In other cases, diasporic experts and research assistants are tasked with organizing their non–Middle Eastern colleagues' research trips to the region, setting up many of their meetings using their personal contacts. Sometimes, diasporic experts travel directly to the region as part of larger research delegations, where once again they are expected to act as "fixers"—using their own networks and family connections to set up meetings with government ministries, civil society organizations, political parties, and occasionally political dissidents (sometimes at great personal risk). In these ways, the diasporic experts can largely curate the US policy community's access to the region—bringing in contacts and networks that even US embassy staff do not always have connections with—determining both whom their white counterparts will meet and what kinds of information will be made "legible" to them.

The diasporic experts also act as intermediaries when elites from the region travel to Washington. Bassem, who criticized the "club" of Egyptian elites who always meet with the US policy experts when they travel to Cairo, told me how he now helps Egyptians who oppose the current military-led government and who are not as well known in Washington, when they come to the city. With the help of several human rights advocacy groups, Bassem coaches his friends and former colleagues on how to speak to US policy makers in order to counter the official Egyptian government narrative in Washington, which is aided by very influential American lobby firms.[25] Bassem sees his work as essential for breaking through the monopoly of voices currently aligned with the current Egyptian government.

Where members of the US security community cannot or choose not to travel to the region or where individuals from the region are unable to travel to Washington, some of the diasporic experts use their own personal narratives and experiences to represent the views of people back home to affectively shape Washington's understanding of the region. For instance, Mehdi Khalaji, an Iran expert who works at the Washington Institute for Near East Policy, a think tank closely associated with AIPAC, touts his story of growing up the "son of an Ayatollah"[26] and training in the seminaries of Qom to legitimate his own polemical analyses against the Iranian government. His personalized narratives also help foster empathy and trust with the DC policy community. Other white experts, particularly those on the right, regularly cite Khalaji as the definitive authority on the clerical system in Iran based on his personal experiences alone.[27] More widely, I observed that first-generation diasporic experts who are religious, ethnic, or sexual minorities or who were persecuted political dissidents in their countries were more likely than their second-generation colleagues to perform this type of affective diplomatic work. Many times, these first-generation diasporic experts used their painful experiences of dislocation, persecution, and violence to "win the hearts" of their US counterparts. In its most problematic forms, these experts purposely eschew the broader historical and political context of the violence they faced back home that would help the US-based audience make better sense of their individualized experiences.[28] Accordingly, their limited narratives tend to further fuel anti-Arab, Islamophobic, and other Orientalist tropes about the people of the region within Washington, which seek to reduce all Muslim men to aggressors and all minorities, women, and members of the LGBTQ+ communities as perpetual victims in need of saving.[29] Similarly, in their work with gay and trans Iranian asylees, Sima Shakhsari found that the refugee narratives that resonated most with Western refugee agencies were those "that inevitably demonize the 'home-country,' thus reproducing the Third World backwardness and barbarism vs. First World freedom narratives."[30] Even those first-generation diasporic experts who want to use their personal experiences to challenge US hegemony are nevertheless asked by their institutions to focus more on their subjective, personal stories when meeting with US government officials rather than assuming the role of the objective regional analyst—an epistemic role reserved for their white counterparts, who benefit from what Uma Kothari calls "the authoritative power of whiteness."[31] At a prominent, closed-door security event I attended in the spring of 2015, Maya, an activist from the region was invited to speak about her experiences during the Arab Spring. Minutes before she went on stage, Maya told me that she wanted to use this opportunity to criticize US policies in the region, as well as make a point about US violence at home against its own populations. However, the moderator of the event focused all of her questions on Maya's life story, leaving no time for her to provide any substantive political commentary. Afterward, Maya expressed frustration with the organizers of the event, feeling that they had intentionally tokenized her experiences rather than allowing her to speak as a regional expert in her own right.

From Tehrangeles to Washington: Contesting Diasporic Politics

Just as diasporic experts use their personal relationships and experiences from the region to give Washington's security community certain kinds of access to the "Middle East," they also act as mediators between various diasporic communities and Washington.

As part of their professional obligations to their think tanks, these experts are required to engage public audiences. Accordingly, most diasporic experts cannot avoid interacting with members of their own diasporic communities at public forums, online, or even during religious or cultural events. Through these interactions, many of these experts use the opportunity to educate or try to persuade their own communities about US policy decisions in the Middle East, trying to overcome common mischaracterizations or misunderstandings about the policy process generally or to defend specific policies. Going back to my opening ethnographic vignette, Jamshid used much of our interview to explain US policy to me as a member of his own diasporic community using registers that were familiar—not only by switching between English and Persian but also by appropriating some of the critical language of the left-wing factions of the Iranian American community. When Jamshid speaks to more conservative groups within our community, as I observed firsthand at several public talks, he uses another set of registers and affective markers, even when making largely the same political observations or analyses. In these ways, these diasporic experts provide essential political but also social knowledge about how Washington functions in practice, helping give these broader political constituencies the tools to better influence policy decisions from the outside in.

Members of these diasporic communities, in turn, seek out these experts to help make their own claims and ideas about the region more legible to the US security community, providing some of the few points of contact (and I would add, accountability) between elites in Washington and nonelite political actors from the region. Some of these demands are articulated through formalized diasporic organizations representing different political factions living in the United States. Such organizations promote specific experts working at established think tanks whose views align with their ideological agendas by inviting them to their conferences, sharing their analyses on social media, and in some cases, offering their members direct contact with these experts as part of their fundraising campaigns. Just as these diasporic organizations can elevate and empower certain experts from their own communities, they can also discipline and discredit others who disagree with their own agendas. For instance, Sayyed, the Egyptian American expert, ran afoul of several Coptic American organizations in DC that are closely aligned with powerful Christian evangelical groups in the United States,[32] because of his more sympathetic stance toward the Muslim Brotherhood. The Coptic groups accused him of serving an Islamist agenda in Washington, and they successfully petitioned several prominent institutions in DC to disinvite him as a speaker.

At other times, these diasporic organizations promote their own in-house experts to try to compete in DC's already saturated marketplace of ideas. For instance, the National Iranian American Council (NIAC) presents itself as a community-based organization that seeks to improve relations between the US and Iran. Its experts frequently use their connections to the Iranian diasporic community to bolster their credibility within Washington, as proxies of a larger political constituency in the US. In other instances, diasporic groups have formed their own think tanks. The Tahrir Institute for Middle East Policy (TIMEP) was formed after the 2011 Arab uprisings by a group of exiled Egyptian activists and second-generation Egyptian American experts, with primary funding from wealthy Egyptians aligned with more oppositional factions within the country. These two organizations alone have widened the field of voices within Washington in a relatively short amount of time. In some instances, they have also directly challenged the dominance of Gulf governments in the geopolitics of funding by promoting diasporic experts who are supported financially by and beholden to members of their own communities in the United States.

Meanwhile, social media platforms, satellite television shows, and online publications have simultaneously "democratized" the space of diasporic politics,[33] allowing individuals within these communities the opportunity to engage but also critique the US imperial apparatus and the role of diasporic experts in Washington within it. Through such media, members of various diasporas bring intense public scrutiny to nearly all aspects of the diasporic experts' backgrounds, views, identities, qualifications (particularly language abilities), regional access, and funding. Most of the diasporic experts I got to know in Washington confessed that their online interactions with members of their own communities were often the most emotionally fraught aspects of their work, as they are forced to confront (and articulate) their moral and ethical obligations to people in the region or else defend their positions vis-à-vis the United States to competing factions within their communities. For instance, Paria, a younger Iranian American expert, told me, "To be Iranian and working on Iran just sucks. You get trolled from both sides as being either a '[Iranian] regime apologist' or a 'mouthpiece for the West.'" Similarly, Karim, an Egyptian American policy expert, explained how he "gets accused of being in collusion with the American government" by vocal, well-known critics and activists in his community who oppose US hegemony in the region. At the same time, he regularly deals with those Egyptians who think he is too critical of the military-led government in Egypt and should therefore keep his "mouth shut." Because of their personal ties to these communities, experts like Karim and Paria cannot fully dismiss these critiques in the same ways that their white counterparts can. Paria told me how each time she goes to the Persian grocery store she prepares herself for the inevitable confrontation with a fellow shopper about her latest article or media appearance.

Collectively, through these kinds of everyday interactions, confrontations, and critiques, diasporic experts contend with the moral and political impact of their work on behalf of various powerful constituencies within Washington in ways that are much more immediate, intimate, and responsive when compared to their white counterparts, who can easily separate themselves affectively and politically from such diasporic communities. And though many of these experts often find these interactions personally irksome, tiring, or even abusive, they also cannot escape the stories, traumas, and political demands that these communities regularly thrust on them. In this way, I would argue that these diasporic experts have become one the few channels through which nonelite actors with personal ties to the region can have their concerns heard within an imperial apparatus that has intentionally ignored the plight of ordinary people in the global Middle East and beyond.

Conclusion

Through this ethnographic study of diasporic security experts from the Middle East, I have tried show that even within the metropole, the US empire operates as a transnational space, where power is contested among a very broad field of elites, including from regions like the Middle East that have long been the targets of US hegemony. In showing this more dynamic view of Washington, I do not seek to deflect critiques of the US empire or whitewash the role of those actors—whether they represent the Global South, North, or both—who help reproduce the logics and violence of empire. On the contrary, I believe that in order to successfully resist or challenge US empire, we need to better contend with how it functions as a multitude of interests, geographies, and imaginaries. We must also understand who is responsible for managing these overlapping though sometimes conflicting terrains. I suggest in this piece that the diasporic experts are one set of actors through which to trace and study these transnational circulations, precisely because of their own liminal, contradictory status between a global Middle East and an expansive, transnational US empire. On a daily basis, experts like Jamshid or Sayyed must simultaneously secure funding from regional governments with their own security agendas, mediate contact between their personal networks in the region and in the United States, all while appealing to increasingly assertive diasporic communities who use these experts to make political demands on other powerful elites in Washington. Among all of these moving parts and contending networks, I drew the most insights into how to begin dismantling the violent logics of empire from observing how more critical diasporic experts navigate these spaces. Such experts are using the existing cleavages and debates in Washington to bring forward the stories and political claims of the very people in the region that US empire has systemically rendered invisible and silent.

Negar Razavi is the public humanities postdoctoral fellow at the Kaplan Institute for the Humanities at Northwestern University. As a political anthropologist, her work examines the intersections of security, expertise, gender, humanitarianism, and US foreign policy in the Middle East. She received her PhD in anthropology from the University of Pennsylvania.

Notes

Without the input, support, generosity, and insights of Samar al-Bulushi, Sahana Ghosh, and Inderpal Grewal, I could never have completed this article. I also want to acknowledge the important work and feedback of the other scholars in this special issue, most especially Deborah A. Thomas, who has been my mentor for many years now. Thank you to all of these women, who have demonstrated how feminist scholarship, mentorship, and solidarity can produce stronger, more critically incisive and relevant work.

1. In this article, I use pseudonyms for all of my interlocutors and, at times, change key biographical details in order to protect their identities given the sensitivity of the topics we discuss. I use the real names of experts when citing their publicly-available work.

2. I refer to these experts as "diasporic" rather than "native" or Middle Eastern American because I wanted a broad enough term that could encompass the many different, transnational positionalities (in terms of citizenship, ethnicity, religion, and race) that these experts occupy. Some of these experts are second-generation immigrants from the Middle East. Others were born and raised in the region and emigrated as adults. Still others lived in Europe for most of their lives, only to make the United States their home for professional reasons.

3. The question of race among people of Middle Eastern and North African descent is a complex one. Though most people from the region are classified as "white" according to the US census and many from the region self-identify as such, critical scholars are increasingly examining the intersecting forces of securitization and racialization that increasingly mark these diverse communities as "nonwhite" (see Khoshneviss, "Inferior White"; Maghbouleh, *Limits of Whiteness*; Zarrugh, "Racialized Political Shock"). Moreover, many of my interlocutors, particularly the younger, second-generation experts who grew up in the aftermath of 9/11, do not self-identify as white.

4. Drezner, *Ideas Industry*.

5. McConnell and Dittmer, "Liminality," 140.

6. Lutz, "Empire Is in the Details"; McGranahan and Collins, *Ethnographies of US Empire*; Thomas, *Political Life*; Vine, *Base Nation*.

7. Simpson, *Mohawk Interruptus*.

8. For instance, Al-Bulushi, "#SomeoneTellCNN"; Tahir, "Ground Was Always in Play"; Li, *Universal Enemy*.

9. McGranahan and Collins, *Ethnographies of US Empire*, 19.

10. Masco, *Theater of Operations*; Gusterson and Besteman, *Insecure American*.

11. Hanieh, *Money, Markets, and Monarchies*; Abboud et al., "Towards a Beirut School"; Bajoghli, *Iran Reframed*.

12. Bayat and Herrera, *Global Middle East*.

13. Gualtieri, *Arab Routes*; Karim, "Iranian Diaspora Studies."

14. Hemmasi, *Tehrangeles Dreaming*.

15. For instance, many of these diasporic experts were born and raised in the United States. Some proudly identify as American and unapologetically support the expansion of US empire. Yet there are others who are far more critical precisely because of their personal experiences as a racialized "Other" in a post-9/11 America. A number of such experts grew up in Europe, as first- or second-generation immigrants, before coming to the United States to work in the foreign policy community as adults—carrying with them a different set of historical legacies of racialized exclu-

sion and inclusion that shape how they interact with and understand security in the US context. An even smaller number of these experts have come directly from the region, in some cases as political asylees or refugees, escaping persecution or as regional elites who have long enjoyed the mobilities uniquely afforded their class.

16. Dabashi, *Brown Skin, White Masks*, 15.

17. Durrani, "Communicating and Contesting Islamophobia"; Z. Grewal, *Islam Is a Foreign Country*; Rana, *Terrifying Muslims*.

18. For instance, the New America Foundation, a well-known think tank in DC, recently launched a "Diversity in National Security" series. In one of their initiatives, they celebrated a group of younger security experts and leaders who "have personal ties to the region and possess unique perspectives that have been integral in re-shaping the discourse around the future of U.S. foreign policy in the Middle East and North Africa." NextGen NatSec, "Next Generation Leaders."

19. Malek, "Paradoxes of Dual Nationality."

20. Williams, Confessore, and Lipton, "Foreign Powers Buy Influence"; Fisher, "How Saudi Arabia Captured Washington."

21. Freeman, *Foreign Funding of Think Tanks*.

22. Since 2014, all three Gulf governments have launched their own think tanks in DC, which have largely worked to advance their official foreign policy agendas in the city through the veneer of "independent" policy research. Several of the major think tanks also have their own affiliated centers and branches in the region, most notably the Carnegie Endowment for International Development's office in Beirut and the Brookings Institution's Doha-based center.

23. Guttman, "Does Israel Buy Influence?"

24. Mearsheimer and Walt, *Israel Lobby and U.S. Foreign Policy*.

25. See the Pecquat, "Egypt Assembles Bipartisan Powerhouse."

26. Khalaji, "Interview: Mehdi Khalaji."

27. See, e.g., Rubin, "Can a Nuclear Iran Be Contained or Deterred?"

28. There are countless examples of this. For instance, Ahmad Batebi, a former student activist in Iran who was detained in 1999 during uprisings, has become a favored expert on Iranian politics and human rights with the Trump administration and its supporters. US Department of State, "U.S. Call for Supporting Human Rights in Iran."

29. Abu-Lughod, *Do Muslim Women Need Saving?*; Amar, *Security Archipelago*; I. Grewal, *Saving the Security State*.

30. Shakhsari, "Queer Time of Death."

31. Kothari, "Agenda for Thinking about 'Race,'" 13.

32. Haddad, "Good Copt, Bad Copt." Also Miray Phillips, a PhD candidate in sociology at the University of Minnesota, is completing her dissertation, tentatively titled "Politics of Persecution: Middle East Christians in US Foreign Policy," which focuses largely on the political role of Coptic Egyptians in shaping US foreign policy.

33. Mottahedeh, *#Iranelection*.

References

Abboud, Samer, Omar S. Dahi, Waleed Hazbun, Nicole Sunday Grove, Coralie Pison Hindawi, Jamil Mouawad, and Sami Hermez. "Towards a Beirut School of Critical Security Studies." *Critical Studies on Security* 6, no. 3 (2018): 273–95. https://doi.org/10.1080/21624887.2018.1522174.

Abu-Lughod, Lila. *Do Muslim Women Need Saving?* Cambridge, MA: Harvard University Press, 2013.

Al-Bulushi, Samar. "#SomeoneTellCNN: Cosmopolitan Militarism in the East African Warscape." *Cultural Dynamics* 31, no. 4 (2019): 323–49. https://doi.org/10.1177/0921374019860933.

Amar, Paul. *The Security Archipelago: Human-Security States, Sexuality Politics, and the End of Neoliberalism.* Durham, NC: Duke University Press, 2013.

Bajoghli, Narges. *Iran Reframed: Anxieties of Power in the Islamic Republic.* Stanford, CA: Stanford University Press, 2019.

Bayat, Asef, and Linda Herrera, eds. *Global Middle East: Into the Twenty-First Century.* Oakland: University of California Press, 2021.

Dabashi, Hamid. *Brown Skin, White Masks.* London: Pluto, 2011.

Drezner, Daniel W. *The Ideas Industry.* New York: Oxford University Press, 2017.

Durrani, Mariam. "Communicating and Contesting Islamophobia." In *Language and Social Justice in Practice*, edited by Netta Avineri, Laura R. Graham, Eric J. Johnson, Robin Conley Riner, and Jonathan Rosa, 44–51. New York: Routledge, 2019.

Fisher, Max. "How Saudi Arabia Captured Washington." *Vox*, March 21, 2016. https://www.vox.com/2016/3/21/11275354/saudi-arabia-gulf-washington.

Freeman, Ben. *Foreign Funding of Think Tanks in America.* Washington, DC: Center for International Policy, January 2020. https://static.wixstatic.com/ugd/3ba8a1_4f06e99f35d4485b801f8dbfe33b6a3f.pdf.

Grewal, Inderpal. *Saving the Security State: Exceptional Citizens in Twenty-First-Century America.* Durham, NC: Duke University Press, 2017.

Grewal, Zareena. *Islam Is a Foreign Country: American Muslims and the Global Crisis of Authority.* New York: New York University Press, 2014.

Gualtieri, Sarah M. A. *Arab Routes: Pathways to Syrian California.* Stanford, CA: Stanford University Press, 2020.

Gusterson, Hugh, and Catherine Besteman, eds. *The Insecure American: How We Got Here and What We Should Do about It.* Berkeley: University of California Press, 2009.

Guttman, Nathan. "Does Israel Buy Influence at US Think Tanks?" *Forward*, September 9, 2014. https://forward.com/opinion/205367/does-israel-buy-influence-at-us-think-tanks/.

Haddad, Yvonne. "Good Copt, Bad Copt: Competing Narratives on Coptic Identity in Egypt and the United States." *Studies in World Christianity* 19, no. 3 (2013): 208–32. https://doi.org/10.3366/swc.2013.0058.

Hanieh, Adam. *Money, Markets, and Monarchies: The Gulf Cooperation Council and the Political Economy of the Contemporary Middle East.* Cambridge: Cambridge University Press, 2018.

Hemmasi, Farzaneh. *Tehrangeles Dreaming: Intimacy and Imagination in Southern California's Iranian Pop Music.* Durham, NC: Duke University Press, 2020.

Karim, Persis. "Introduction: Iranian Diaspora Studies." *Iranian Studies* 46, no. 1 (2013): 49–52. https://doi.org/10.1080/00210862.2012.740896.

Khalaji, Mehdi. "Interview: Mehdi Khalaji," by Elizabeth Dickinson. *Foreign Policy*, July 27, 2009. https://foreignpolicy.com/2009/07/27/interview-mehdi-khalaji/.

Khoshneviss, Hadi. "The Inferior White: Politics and Practices of Racialization of People from the Middle East in the US." *Ethnicities* 19, no. 1 (2019): 117–35. https://doi.org/10.1177/1468796818798481.

Kothari, Uma. "An Agenda for Thinking about 'Race' in Development." *Progress in*

Development Studies 6, no. 1 (2006): 9–23. https://doi.org/10.1191/1464993406ps1 24oa.

Li, Darryl. *The Universal Enemy: Jihad, Empire, and the Challenge of Solidarity.* Stanford, CA: Stanford University Press, 2019.

Lutz, Catherine. "Empire Is in the Details." *American Ethnologist* 33, no. 4 (2006): 593–611. https://doi.org/10.1525/ae.2006.33.4.593.

Maghbouleh, Neda. *The Limits of Whiteness: Iranian Americans and the Everyday Politics of Race.* Stanford, CA: Stanford University Press, 2017.

Malek, Amy. "Paradoxes of Dual Nationality: Geopolitical Constraints on Multiple Citizenship in the Iranian Diaspora." *Middle East Journal* 73, no. 4 (2019): 531–54. https://doi.org/10.3751/73.4.11.

Masco, Joseph. *The Theater of Operations: National Security Affect from the Cold War to the War on Terror.* Durham, NC: Duke University Press, 2014.

McConnell, Fiona, and Jason Dittmer. "Liminality and the Diplomacy of the British Overseas Territories: An Assemblage Approach." *Environment and Planning D: Society and Space* 36, no. 1 (2018): 139–58. https://doi.org/10.1177 /0263775817733479.

McGranahan, Carole, and John F. Collins, eds. *Ethnographies of U.S. Empire.* Durham, NC: Duke University Press, 2018.

Mearsheimer, John J., and Stephen M. Walt. *The Israel Lobby and U.S. Foreign Policy.* New York: Farrar, Straus and Giroux, 2008.

Mottahedeh, Negar. *#Iranelection: Hashtag Solidarity and the Transformation of Online Life.* Stanford, CA: Stanford University Press. 2015.

NextGen NatSec. "2020 Middle Eastern and North African American National Security and Foreign Policy Next Generation Leaders." #NextGenNatSec Expert Lists, September 8, 2020. https://nextgennatsec.com/2020/12/16/nextgen natsec-mena-amercan-2020/.

Pecquat, Julian. "Egypt Assembles Bipartisan Powerhouse Lobbying Team for Post-Trump Era." Foreign Lobby Report, November 11, 2020. https://www .foreignlobby.com/2020/11/11/egypt-assembles-bipartisan-powerhouse-lobbying -team-for-post-trump-era/.

Rana, Junaid Akram. *Terrifying Muslims: Race and Labor in the South Asian Diaspora.* Durham, NC: Duke University Press, 2011.

Rubin, Michael. "Can a Nuclear Iran Be Contained or Deterred?" *Critical Threats,* November 5, 2008. https://www.criticalthreats.org/analysis/can-a-nuclear-iran -be-contained-or-deterred.

Shakhsari, Sima. "The Queer Time of Death: Temporality, Geopolitics, and Refugee Rights." *Sexualities* 17, no. 8 (2014): 998–1015. https://doi.org/10.1177 /1363460714552261.

Simpson, Audra. *Mohawk Interruptus: Political Life across the Borders of Settler States.* Durham, NC: Duke University Press, 2014.

Tahir, Madiha. "The Ground Was Always in Play." *Public Culture,* no. 81 (2017): 5–16. https://doi.org/10.1215/08992363-3644373.

Thomas, Deborah A. *Political Life in the Wake of the Plantation: Sovereignty, Witnessing, Repair.* Durham, NC: Duke University Press, 2019.

United States Department of State. "U.S. Call for Supporting Human Rights in Iran." Briefing, September 28, 2018. https://2017-2021.state.gov/u-s-call-for -supporting-human-rights-in-iran/index.html.

Vine, David. *Base Nation: How U.S. Military Bases Abroad Harm America and the World.* New York: Metropolitan, 2015.

Williams, Brooke, Nicholas Confessore, and Eric Lipton. "Foreign Powers Buy Influence at Think Tanks." *New York Times*, September 6, 2014. http://www.nytimes.com/2014/09/07/us/politics/foreign-powers-buy-influence-at-think-tanks.html.

Zarrugh, Amina. "Racialized Political Shock: Arab American Racial Formation and the Impact of Political Events." *Ethnic and Racial Studies* 39, no. 15 (2016): 2722–39. https://doi.org/10.1080/01419870.2016.1171368.